JACKSON & LEE

JACKSON & LEE
LEGENDS *in* GRAY

THE PAINTINGS OF MORT KÜNSTLER

TEXT BY JAMES I. ROBERTSON, JR.

RUTLEDGE HILL PRESS

Nashville, Tennessee

For Deborah,
the perfect wife

Published in Nashville, Tennessee, by Rutledge Hill Press, 211 Seventh Avenue North, Nashville, Tennessee 37219. Distributed in Canada by H. B. Fenn and Company Ltd., Mississauga, Ontario.

Jacket and text design by Bruce Gore, Gore Studios, Inc.

Typography by D&T/Bailey Typesetting, Inc., Nashville, Tennessee.

Color separations and electronic file preparation by Capitol Engraving Company, Nashville, Tennessee.

Library of Congress Cataloging-in-Publication Data

Künstler, Mort.
    Jackson and Lee : legends in gray / the paintings of Mort Künstler ; text by James I. Robertson, Jr.
        p.   cm.
    Includes bibliographical references (p.   ) and index.
    ISBN 1-55853-333-8 (hardcover)
    1. Generals—Confederate States of America—Biography.
2. Generals—Confederate States of America—Portraits.
3. Confederate States of America. Army—Biography. 4. Lee, Robert E. (Robert Edward), 1807–1870. 5. Lee, Robert E. (Robert Edward), 1807–1870—Portraits. 6. Jackson, Stonewall, 1824–1863. 7. Jackson, Stonewall, 1824–1863—Portraits. 8. United States—History—Civil War, 1861–1865—Campaigns. 9. United States—History—Civil War, 1861–1865—Art and the war. I. Robertson, James I. II. Title.
E467.K86   1995
973.7'42—dc20   95–34556
                                                                  CIP

Printed in the United States of America.

1 2 3 4 5 6 7 8 9—99 98 97 96 95

Photo Credits: *Page 19*. Lee's field glasses with case, hat, revolver, and sword belt. The Museum of the Confederacy, Richmond, Virginia. Photograph by Katherine Wetzel. *Page 21*. Lee's revolver. Courtesy of Arlington House, Robert E. Lee Memorial, administered by the National Park Service, Arlington, Virginia. *Page 26*. Lee's frock coat. The Museum of the Confederacy, Richmond, Virginia. Photograph by Katherine Wetzel. *Page 30*. Lee's saddle. The Museum of the Confederacy, Richmond, Virginia. Photograph by Katherine Wetzel. *Page 52*. Jackson's revolver. The Museum of the Confederacy, Richmond, Virginia. Photograph by Katherine Wetzel. *Page 69*. Jackson's kepi. Courtesy of VMI Museum collection, Lexington, Virginia. *Page 78*. Lee's hat. The Museum of the Confederacy, Richmond, Virginia. Photograph by Katherine Wetzel. *Page 85*. Jackson's brigade flag carried at First Manassas. Courtesy of VMI Museum collection, Lexington, Virginia. *Page 98*. New Testament with bullet hole. Eleanor S. Brockenbrough Library, the Museum of the Confederacy, Richmond, Virginia. Photograph by Katherine Wetzel. *Page 100*. Jackson's field desk. VMI Museum collection, Lexington, Virginia. Photograph by David J. Eicher/Well-Traveled Images. *Page 110*. Jackson's raincoat. Courtesy of VMI Museum collection, Lexington, Virginia. *Page 115*. Lee's headquarters flag. The Museum of the Confederacy, Richmond, Virginia. Photograph by Katherine Wetzel. *Page 123*. Model 1855 Harpers Ferry rifle. Gettysburg National Military Park, Gettysburg, Pennsylvania. From *The Civil War: Lee Takes Command*, photograph by Larry Sherer, © 1984 Time-Life Books. *Page 142*. Union drum. From the collection of Russell W. Fay, Milwaukee, Wisconsin. Photograph by David J. Eicher/Well-Traveled Images. *Page 147*. Haversack. The Museum of the Confederacy, Richmond, Virginia. Photograph by Katherine Wetzel. *Page 155*. Bronze Cross of Honor. Courtesy of New Market Battlefield Historical Park, New Market, Virginia. *Page 167*. Lee's surrender sword. The Museum of the Confederacy, Richmond, Virginia. Photograph by Katherine Wetzel.

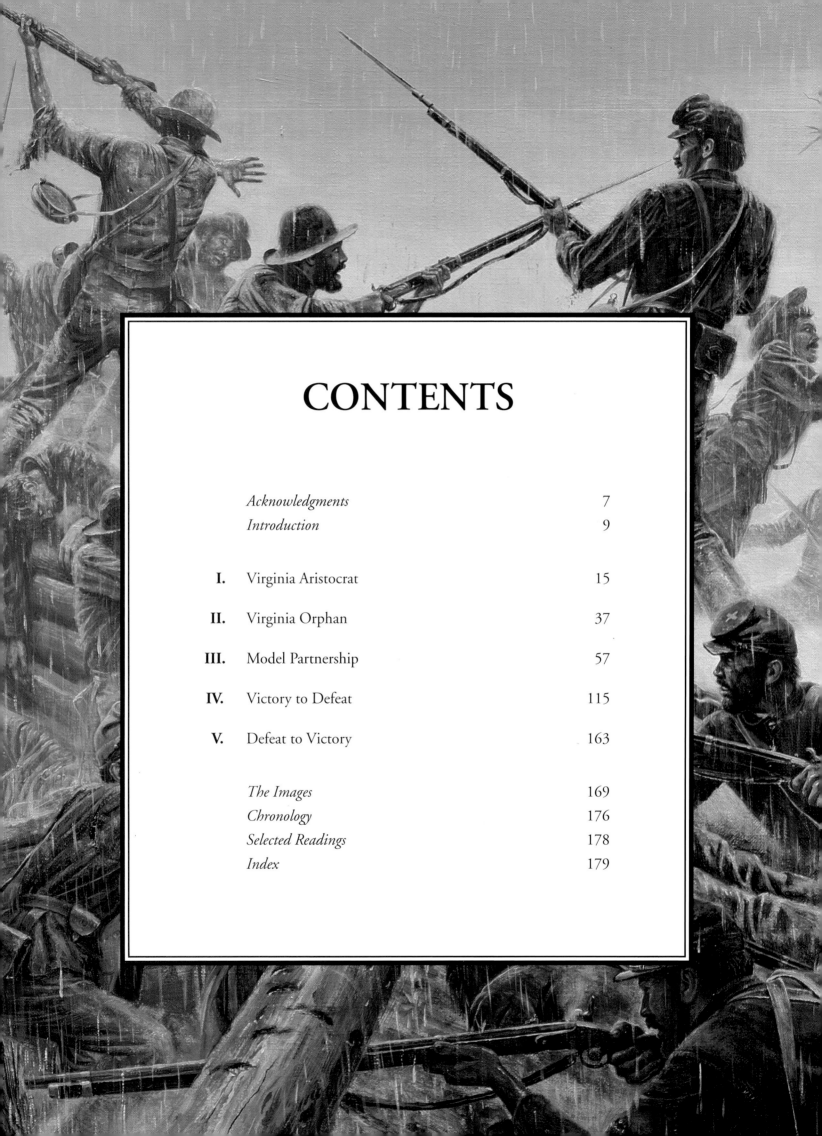

CONTENTS

ACKNOWLEDGMENTS

IT HAS BEEN SAID THAT COMING out with a book is like giving birth to a child. I have never experienced the latter but can attest to the pain and ecstasy of the former. Without the help of an army of people, both Union and Confederate, this book would never have come to be.

Larry Stone, president of Rutledge Hill Press, was encouraging right from the start, and his leadership and advice throughout the project was invaluable. I thank him for his foresight, his patience, and all the help that has made the creation of this book easier.

I am deeply honored to have a sparkling and illuminative text by Alumni Distinguished Professor James I. Robertson Jr. of Virginia Tech, the foremost authority on Stonewall Jackson. Getting to know him and his charming wife, Libba, has indeed been a pleasure. In addition to his friendship, he has given me all kinds of data such as weather conditions, times of day, events and personalities to help ensure the historical accuracy of the paintings in this book.

It is impossible to list all the historians with whom I have consulted. All have been of immeasurable help. Special thanks are due to author-historian Rod Gragg; Pulitzer Prize–winning author-historian Professor James McPherson of Princeton University, Steven Silvia, author and publisher of North South Trader's Civil War; Lt. Col. Keith Gibson, director of the Virginia Military Institute Museum; Senior Historian Kathy Georg Harrison and historians John Heiser and Bob Prosperi of the Gettysburg National Military Park; Ben Ritter and Rebecca Ebert of the Handley Library, Winchester, Virginia; Pat Jennings, former manager of Stonewall Jackson's Headquarters Museum; Michael Gore, executive director of Belle Grove, Middletown, Virginia; and Brandon H. Beck, director of the Civil War Institute, Shenandoah University. My gratitude to David Künstler, my son, wildlife management specialist and naturalist for the New York City Department of Parks and Recreation, who has always given me the most accurate information regarding trees, wildflowers, and birds.

I am indebted to Richard Lynch, director of Hammer Galleries, New York City, who "discovered" me and gave me my first one-man show at the gallery in 1977. My sincere appreciation to him for bringing the exhibition "Jackson & Lee—Legends in Gray" to the gallery in October 1995, my tenth show at Hammer, marking a very happy twenty-year association.

My good friends, Ted and Mary Sutphen of American Print Gallery in Gettysburg, the publisher of my limited edition prints, have been of immeasurable help and I cannot thank them enough. I look forward to continuing our personal and professional relationship for many years to come.

My daughter, Jane Künstler, with the help of Paula McEvoy, has taken over the burden of running a busy studio, allowing me the time to do what I like best—paint. I am deeply indebted to them both and could not function without them.

And, of course, my heartfelt thanks to my beautiful wife, Deborah, who has been there for me throughout my career. She has truly been the "wind beneath my wings."

INTRODUCTION

IT IS SO EASY TO OVERLOOK THE human element in war. Hostilities usually take the form of two hosts struggling for supremacy in an inanimate void. Battle maps depict opposing armies as different colored arrows pointing hither and yon. Casualties are merely numbers. Valor and suffering at most are footnotes.

Sometimes the nature of a struggle and the behavior of its participants have a dominance that eclipses the normal facets of warfare. Men rise to heights as indelible as they are immeasurable. Uncommon valor becomes a common virtue.

The American Civil War possessed those ingredients. A great experiment in democracy was in crisis. What the Founding Fathers had designated as the "United States" existed in name only. Starting in December 1860, eleven Southern states, weary of the agitations for change, expressed their right of freedom by withdrawing from the Union. However, secession seemed to repudiate the basic American tenet of majority rule. So two distinct sections, each claiming to be expressing American principles, resorted to arms with unbending determination.

What resulted was the greatest event in American history. More men and women died in those four years than in all of our other wars *combined.* The Civil War is the line of demarcation between the old and the new nation. That struggle defined once and for all the future destiny of a United States in fact.

It is all sometimes difficult to grasp. Seeing the war in its full impact, Walker Percy wrote, "is like a man walking away from a mountain. The bigger it is, the farther he's got to go before he can see it. Then one day he looks back and there it is, this colossal thing lying across his past."

Nowhere else in our annals do we find a larger number of memorable figures than those who embodied the Civil War. The list begins at the top with Presidents Abraham Lincoln and Jefferson Davis, descends through some of the most superb military leaders America has produced, and comes to rest on the broad base of Johnny Rebs and Billy Yanks. Those young citizen-soldiers fought and died for something larger than their lives, and in the end they gave us the assurance that whenever America faces an emergency of gigantic proportion, its common folk can and will surmount the test with their strength.

In the pantheon of American soldiers, none stands taller than Gens. Robert Edward Lee and Thomas Jonathan "Stonewall" Jackson. They now seem larger than life. When considering Lee and Jackson, eyes seem to lift. So does the mind. The very words those men used—*gentleman, duty, valor, honor*—have a quaint sound in these times because they have become unfamiliar terms. People who say that Lee and Jackson did not really exist make that statement because no one like them exists now.

Several of Europe's most respected generals have acknowledged openly the preeminence of the two Confederate field commanders. Sir Garnet Joseph Wolseley, who met Lee on several occasions during the Civil War, later wrote: "I never felt my own individual insignificance more keenly than I did in his presence. I have met many of the great men of my time, but Lee alone impressed me with the feeling that I was in the presence of a man who was cast in a grander mould, and made of different and of finer metal than all other men."

Lord Frederick Roberts stated in 1914: "In my opinion Stonewall Jackson was one of the greatest natural geniuses the world ever saw. I will go even further than that—as a campaigner in the field he never had a superior. In some respects I doubt whether he had an equal."

A trained soldier and experienced politician, President Jefferson Davis (1808–89) became a lonely nationalist who devoted all of his energies toward gaining independence for a Southern confederation. He was erect and handsome, with unwavering devotion to his cause but without the popular admiration that might have made him more successful.

Generals Lee and Jackson were Virginians, West Pointers, Mexican War heroes, and accomplished soldiers. They fought for the Southern Confederacy because in the nineteenth century the state that had nurtured them was their motherland. Working in concert for only a year, they shaped war as no two commanders ever have. Yet theirs was a strange partnership of the patrician and the plebeian. They were of different generations and vastly different cultures.

The greatness of Lee and Jackson came from their similarities. Jackson regarded Lee with admiration and respect merged into one. Extracting such strong feeling from Jackson required that the recipient be not only a soldier of front-rank genius, but a good and pious man as well. Jackson saw these qualities in Lee, and his esteem for his chieftain remained unwavering from beginning to end.

Both commanders came quickly to the defense of one another against unfounded criticism. At the outset of their association, Jackson heard someone mention that Lee tended to be slow. "Old Jack" quickly snapped in reply: "General Lee is *not* slow. No one knows the weight upon his heart—his great responsibilities. He is commander in chief, and he knows that, if an army is lost, it cannot be replaced. No! . . . If you ever hear that said of General Lee, I beg you will contradict it in my name. I have known General Lee for five and twenty years. He is cautious. He ought to be."

Equally bold in conception and in fierceness of execution, neither general hesitated to take risks for the larger goal of ultimate victory. Each possessed the same selfless devotion to his native land and its fight for independence; each had the same abiding faith in God's blessing on that land.

He entered the presidency with civil war waiting for him. The tall, thin, and homely Abraham Lincoln (1809–65) met his responsibilities squarely. At the moment of triumph, he became the first American president to be assassinated. Historians continue to rank him as the greatest of our chief executives.

Jackson fell at the midway point of the war, after a two-year career filled with brilliant successes. Lee continued to lead the army that he had molded. Under his guidance, it had arguably become man-for-man the greatest fighting force ever seen on the continent. However, as the Civil War broadened and in time controlled those who initially had sought to control it, Lee found that he was no longer fighting with just another army. The great force he led was a personally designed, hand-wrought sword that could not continue to fend off the machine-tooled Northern weapons that kept coming in incalculable numbers. In the end, with Jackson dead for the cause, Lee had the harder task of accompanying the cause to its death.

Sometimes there is honor in tragedy and inspiration in defeat. Lee and Jackson most seem to embody those truths in the American pantheon. That explains why tens of thousands of people with

a respect for history look back on "Marse Robert" and "Old Jack" in wonder and with esteem.

Those feelings characterize the work of Mort Künstler. Of all artists in America, he has concentrated the most on the military careers of the two most prominent Southern generals. Künstler succeeds in portraying those commanders as living beings caught in time, in poses both noble and mystical. His portraits of other leaders reflect the aura of their personalities. In the battle paintings can be seen brave men displaying the full gamut of emotions: courage and shock, patriotism and pain, the will to push ahead, the acceptance of death.

Künstler's extraordinary talent with the brush and his reverential attention to accuracy and detail have made him the premier historical artist of our time. This collection of art can but reinforce that reputation. It is a tribute to all men of blue and gray, but especially to two Christian soldiers who epitomize the "legends in gray."

PART

I

*Virginia
Aristocrat*

VIRGINIA ARISTOCRAT

By MAY 1863 THE CIVIL WAR was entering its third year. Union and Confederacy were then waging an all-out contest. Twenty-four months of combat had brought growth only to the casualty lists. Federal armies were making inroads in Tennessee and other parts of the western theater, but in the East, Union efforts in Virginia had been one failure after another. As a new season of campaigning began, the unanswered question seemed to be which would be exhausted first: Southern resources or Northern morale?

The key to the answer lay with two Virginians, Confederate Gens. Robert E. Lee and Thomas J. "Stonewall" Jackson. They met briefly for the first time in the Mexican War and had no contact again until civil war brought them together. It was June 1862 before they came into direct personal association. Thereafter, they were a military team unseen in the annals of warfare. The Southern nation's president, Jefferson Davis, would later say in wonder: "They supplemented each other, and, together, with fair opportunity, they were absolutely invincible."

So brilliant a military association was not a natural welding of similar personalities; far from it. Lee and Jackson were seventeen years apart in age and a world apart in social background. One man was charismatic and extremely courteous; the other wrapped in silence and an overpowering faith in God. The dissimilarities between the two were at least equal to their commonality. Still, even though they might be days apart in distance and communication, the Tidewater aristocrat and the mountain orphan worked in concert to a remarkable degree.

Lee never had a lieutenant so quick to grasp his thoughts, so reliable in executing his strategy, and—when on his own—so capable of taking care of himself while he marched and fought toward a grand purpose. Not one harsh word passed between the two. Their relations were as formal as they were affectionate. In Lee and Jackson, one writer concluded, "integrity met integrity."

Some differences between them were pronounced. Lee maintained open communications with his principal lieutenants. Jackson kept his own counsel with respect to his subordinates. Many of those division and brigade commanders misinterpreted Jackson's penchant for secrecy as distrust of his officers—a situation that promoted blind obedience or transfer elsewhere. On the other hand, when Jackson dealt with Lee, he was the most candid of subalterns.

Attitude toward discipline was another diversity between them. Lee was reluctant to hurt the feelings of an officer who seemed to be doing his best. He tolerated a number of incompetents for too long. The kindness of Lee's heart therefore had occasionally impaired the efficiency of Lee's army.

Jackson, in contrast, was stern and remorseless in disciplinary matters. His sole thought in the Civil War was to engage and crush the heathen waging war against his country. If an officer performed below par in the process, Jackson thrust him aside with as little ceremony as removing a private from the ranks.

Technically, Jackson was below Lee's other corps commanders in seniority. Gen. James Longstreet had admirable qualities: he was steady, dependable, every inch a soldier. Yet Jackson possessed military assets that no other Civil War general had displayed. Dauntless, brilliant, imbued with even greater aggressive instincts than were inherent in Lee, he rapidly ascended to the

AT LEFT:
Lee was the son of an American Revolution hero, a high-ranking graduate of West Point, and a soldier with thirty years' experience when civil war began. Opposed to both the institution of slavery and the use of secession as a political weapon, Lee cast his lot with the Confederacy because his beloved country —Virginia—had taken that course.

NEXT PAGE:
A major criticism of Lee was his failure to develop and use a large staff. Never in the war did his "inner family" exceed seven men. For most of the war the Army of Northern Virginia's staff consisted of Col. Walter H. Taylor, a Norfolk banker with a photographic memory.

heights of a military genius. Lee knew it. Jackson might be a subordinate, but in Lee's eyes he had risen to an equal.

Some of Jackson's soldiers believed that, but most Southern contemporaries disagreed. Lee the army commander occupied an exalted position that no one else in the Confederate States approached. By the last year's fighting in Virginia, it can be said—as indeed many did say—that Lee *was* the Confederacy for the army ranks and civilian population alike. In retrospect, the life of Robert Edward Lee seems incredibly blameless. He has been hailed as "the incarnation of the cavalier tradition so dear to the southern heart." A recent biographer concluded of Lee: "He redeemed many moments and brought grace to otherwise grim circumstances."

Lee was the very embodiment of all that was good in the Confederate States of America. As a soldier and as a person, Lee was the determining factor in the course of the Civil War in Virginia. Just as his brilliance kept the Southern nation alive in the last three years of that struggle, his vision at Appomattox shaped the future of the American nation forged by that conflict.

A product of "Old America"—of aristocracy in decline—Lee was born in January 1807 at Stratford estate in the Virginia Tidewater. The Lee family was a combination of some of the finest colonial stock. Robert Lee's forebears were prime actors in the movement toward American freedom in the eighteenth century, and two were signers of the Declaration of Independence. Lee's mother was Ann Carter; his father Henry "Light-Horse Harry" Lee, was a Revolutionary War hero and Virginia governor.

At the time of Robert's birth the family fortunes had largely evaporated because of the

A reporter for the London Times *thought Lee's manner "calm and stately," his presence "impressive and imposing." The general was so kind and courteous that "a child thrown among a knot of strangers would inevitably be drawn to him . . . and would run to claim his protection."*

father's brash financial ways. Henry Lee died impoverished during Robert's youth. The lad grew up in a modest Alexandria, Virginia, townhouse. Still, the careful tutelage of his mother instilled in Lee the attributes of duty, obligation, and respect.

West Point offered young Lee an opportunity for a solid education and a soldier's life. He accepted appointment from President James Monroe and in 1825 entered the U.S. Military Academy. Good behavior, an above-average academic background, plus a mind that was both quick and precise, served Lee well as a cadet. His four-year record contains no demerits—an achievement that remains unequaled at West Point. He became corps adjutant, the highest cadet rank at the academy.

After Lee graduated number two in a class of forty-six, one of his friends openly confessed that "no youth or man so united the qualities that win warm friendship and command high respect. . . . His correctness of demeanor and attention to all duties, personal and official, and a dignity as much a part of himself as the elegance of his person, gave him a superiority that everyone acknowledged in his heart."

High standing won Lee appointment to the Corps of Engineers, the army's smallest and most elite branch. This was a time when the Congress gave strong support to public and military projects. Lee's first assignments were to oversee work on several coastal fortifications. From Fort Pulaski, the principal defense of the Savannah River in Georgia, he moved to Fort Monroe at

Lee acquired Traveller, his famous mount, in the first year of the war. The horse served his owner faithfully and without injury through the war. He survived the general by only eight months. Traveller is buried just a few feet from Lee outside the chapel of Washington and Lee University.

the mouth of Hampton Roads, Virginia, and then to Fort Hamilton, which guarded the entrance to the harbor of New York City.

The death of his mother in 1829 left Lieutenant Lee with an inheritance of ten slaves and a distinguished family name. Two years later, he married Mary Custis, whose grandfather had been the adopted son of George Washington. Mary was an only child; hence, she was in line to inherit Arlington, the imposing Custis mansion across the Potomac River from Washington. This became Lee's home when he was not on military duty elsewhere. Robert and Mary Lee would have seven children, most of whom were raised at Arlington.

Throughout his military career, Lee was an extraordinarily handsome man. He stood five feet, eleven inches tall, with medium build, black hair, and brown eyes. He rode a horse as if born on it, and when he walked into a room, people instinctively turned to study the Virginian. Many considered Lee the most imposing individual ever to wear the uniform of an American soldier.

He was serving as a harbor engineer on the Mississippi River at Saint Louis when the Mexican War beckoned. Lee joined army commander Winfield Scott's staff and became a trusted member of the general's small circle of advisers. It was Lee who suggested the strategies that resulted in climactic American victories at Cerro Gordo and Chapultepec. At the end of the war, Lee held three brevet promotions for gallantry. General Scott openly announced: "American success in Mexico was largely due to the skill, valor, and undaunted energy of Robert E. Lee. . . . He was the very best soldier I ever saw in the field."

Lee would have been the last person to magnify his deeds. He had shown clear thinking, prompt action, and endurance under fire. Many lessons in command he had acquired from the general who was his mentor.

A return to peacetime engineering duties took Lee to Fort Carroll in Baltimore harbor. In 1853 the War Department underscored Lee's worth by naming him superintendent of West

LEE'S SWORD BELT, FIELD GLASSES, REVOLVER, AND HAT

Point. There he met many of the officers-to-be with whom and against whom he would fight a decade later. The colonel had to wrestle with the problems of several cadets. Twice his nephew Fitzhugh Lee came close to dismissal. Another cadet, "Curly" Whistler, preferred drawing to studies and eventually left the academy. Yet artist James McNeill Whistler never forgot Lee's many kindnesses.

Secretary of War Jefferson Davis then transferred Lee from staff to line by appointing him lieutenant colonel of the Army's flagship unit, the Second U.S. Cavalry. Lee's reputation as a conscientious and fair-minded officer resulted in his being named regularly to serve on courts-martial. Such tasks carried him to posts all over the country.

The death in 1857 of his father-in-law, George Washington Parke Custis, forced Lee to take a protracted leave of absence. He returned to Arlington as executor of a large estate in all but total disarray. Lee found it a sad homecoming, far from the gay and prospering abode he had known. Worst of all, Mrs. Lee was so crippled by arthritis that she was virtually an invalid. Lee's wife remained in that condition the remainder of her life.

For two years the army officer worked at unraveling deeds, wills, business contracts, incomplete financial sheets, and the like. Much still remained to be done with the Custis estate when, in October 1859, John Brown and a small band of abolitionists seized the federal arsenal at Harpers Ferry, Virginia. A detachment of marines was the only contingent of troops in Washington at the time. Army colonel Lee took command of the marines and moved at once to quell the disturbance. Also accompanying Lee to Harpers Ferry was a young aide and fellow Virginian, J. E. B. "Jeb" Stuart.

Brown and his followers, with thirteen hostages, barricaded themselves in a small engine house. Marines stormed the building, a quick exchange of gunfire occurred, and the raid was over. All of Brown's men were killed or captured. None of the hostages received injury. Lee had performed quickly and efficiently.

By the following year, he was in command of the First U.S. Cavalry in Texas. Yet as the national sky darkened and peals of secessionist thunder rolled from the South, Lee became increasingly worried. To one of his children he wrote: "A Union that can only be maintained by swords and bayonets, and in which strife and civil war are to take the place of brotherly love and kindness, has no charm for me. . . . If the Union is dissolved, and the Government disrupted, I shall return to my native State and share the miseries of my people, and save in defence will draw my sword on none."

The crisis worsened. Colonel Lee felt an obligation to join his family at Arlington. Confederates bombarded Fort Sumter, South Carolina. War became a reality. Within days, Lee received a summons from his fellow Virginian and close friend, Winfield Scott. The general in chief of the army was instrumental in the Federal government's tendering to Lee command of the principal Union forces in the East.

Lee found himself in a painful dilemma. He was strongly committed to the U.S. Constitution and to the Union; he had given thirty years of his life to the U.S. Army. Now the nation had become a political hybrid that appeared to be held together only by bayonets. Lee wanted nothing of that. Yet as shouting progressed to shooting, he realized that Virginia would be the first target of Federal might. An ancestral obligation to his state, coupled with a strong regionalism at a time when the "United States" existed in name only, proved to be overriding persuasions.

On April 20, 1861, he submitted his resignation from the army. "Lee, you have made the greatest mistake of your life," Scott told him sadly. "But I feared it would be so." The two men never saw each other again.

The daughter of a Northern friend wrote Lee at this time and asked for his autograph. He responded with a moving explanation for the course he had taken. "I can say in sincerity that I bear animosity against no one. Wherever the blame may be, the fact is that we are in the midst of a fratricidal war. I must side with my section of the country. I cannot raise my hand against my birthplace, my home, my children. I should like, above all things, that our difficulties might be peaceably arranged, and still trust that a merciful

God, whom I know will not unnecessarily afflict us, may yet allay the fury for war."

Three days later, Lee arrived in Richmond to accept command of Virginia's armed forces. He impressed one and all by appearance as well as bearing. A staff officer recalled his first meeting with Lee. "Admirably proportioned, of graceful and dignified carriage, with strikingly handsome features, bright and penetrating eyes, his iron-gray hair closely cut, his face cleanly shaved except for a mustache, he appeared every inch a soldier and a man born to command."

The principles that had spawned the sectional conflict were not important to Lee. He had no stake in the institution of slavery (he was then engaged in the "distasteful" task of manumitting the slaves of his deceased father-in-law). Similarly, Lee had no confidence in secession as a viable political weapon. As a soldier, he had simply reacted to coercion of his native land by a federal government that Southern leaders believed no longer was the image of the Revolutionary fathers.

His accomplishments notwithstanding, there was about Lee a pronounced shyness. He avoided crowds and individuals he did not know well. His public career spanned the better part of a half century, yet his public utterances were few and incredibly brief. In the only speech he gave in the

entire Civil War, Lee closed his three-sentence acceptance of commander of Virginia's military buildup with the words: "Trusting in Almighty God, an approving conscience, and the aid of my fellow citizens, I devote myself to the service of my native state, in whose behalf I alone will ever draw my sword."

The same purity of patriotism that had inspired his father, uncles, and cousins in the American Revolution also motivated not only Robert Lee but his three sons as well. Two became Confederate generals, while the youngest rose to the rank of captain.

Meanwhile, Union officials confiscated the Lee-Custis mansion. In a blatant act of vengeance for Lee's casting his lot with the South, the Federal secretary of war authorized Arlington to be converted into a soldier burial ground. The estate would ultimately become the nation's largest national cemetery.

The fifty-four-year-old Virginia commander instantly displayed great powers of organization. In those early days of the war, Lee sought four things: the help of the Almighty, time to prepare, weapons to use, and understanding on the part of the Southern people that this war was going to call for deep sacrifice.

Within two months, Lee mobilized forty thousand troops, thirty field batteries, and fifteen coastal defense batteries. He used Virginia Military Institute cadets as drill instructors; he placed proven or promising officers in command of strategic sites around the perimeter of the state. Those locales also became rendezvous camps for the thousands of recruits flocking into the army.

Lee placed the Old Dominion in a better state of preparedness than anyone imagined possible. It was he alone who crafted the framework of an army that met and stopped the first Union invasion in July near Manassas Junction. By then, however, Lee had moved to new and more agonizing duties.

After Virginia units were integrated into Confederate service, Lee became a full general and informal adviser to Confederate President

Between Lee and his soldiers was a mutual and remarkable affection. An officer who saw him often during the war declared that Lee "assumed no airs of superior authority. . . . His bearing was that of a friend having a common interest in a common venture with the person addressed. . . . He was less of an actor than any man I ever saw."

For the Confederates, the night of May 31, 1862, was chaos mixed with gloom. Attacks at Seven Pines had failed to dislodge the Union army, and Gen. Joseph E. Johnston, the Southern commander, was seriously wounded. As President Davis and his military adviser made their way from the battlefield through the jam of ambulances and debris toward Richmond, Davis suddenly turned in the saddle and told Lee that he would be the new leader of the Confederate army.

Jefferson Davis. The professional soldier soon discovered that it is terrible to have to live up to high expectations. Yet he suffered the "birth defect" of being the son of Henry Lee. Always so much was expected.

A year would pass with Lee basically locked in administrative functions. He became a high-ranking figure subjected to waves of public criticism. It was the duties, not the performance, that brought Lee such unpopularity.

His first major chore as a presidential trouble shooter came in the autumn. Lee traveled to the mountains of western Virginia to try to iron out differences between three brigadier generals, each with separate commands, overlapping responsibilities, and clashing egos. Lee did not have the stern, no-nonsense demeanor needed to rectify an internal squabble in the face of advancing Union forces. Advising without authority, his mission was a failure. Federals easily occupied most of the territory in question. Lee returned to Richmond with visible signs of a graying beard and with an uncomplimentary nickname: "Evacuating Lee."

A week later, Davis dispatched Lee to inspect—and, if necessary, to improve—the coastal fortifications below North Carolina, especially at Charleston. The engineer found Confederate defenses insufficient and overextended. He ordered the scattered barrier islands along the coast abandoned and a solid chain of defensive works constructed several miles up the rivers on the mainland.

This was well-reasoned strategy. However, many influential coastal families were forced to flee inland as refugees. Their loud wails of protest echoed all the way to Richmond. In addition, Lee directed all able-bodied men in the Charleston area to work on the construction of earthworks and gun emplacements. Gentlemen unaccustomed to such menial labor added their voices to the atmosphere of unrest. Lee acquired a second unflattering sobriquet: "the King of Spades."

Davis recalled Lee to the capital in March 1862 and appointed the Virginian to take "control of military operations"—to be in effect the

LEE'S FROCK COAT

of being part of the high command without a command. He advised while other generals fought; he was an involuntary administrator who longed for field command.

Still, Lee proved to be a gifted military overseer and referee. Tact, understanding, and positive relationships with widely varying personalities began to make him an almost indispensable element in the military hierarchy. For example, Lee often found himself squarely between the proud and highly sensitive Davis and the proud and highly sensitive General Johnston. That Lee kept the two men focused more on the enemy and less on their sharp differences of opinion was no mean accomplishment. Lee's relationships with Davis were always cordial because Lee confided willingly in his commander in chief. Johnston never learned that basic duty.

With Johnston totally preoccupied by McClellan's peninsula offensive against Richmond and Davis too distracted by a myriad of national concerns, Lee was free to deal with other Confederate forces in Virginia. His tact and common sense served him well. Lee opened communications with one of the most secretive commanders in American history: Gen. Stonewall Jackson, commanding Southern troops in the Shenandoah Valley. The letter exchange became regular, and it was always friendly.

It was the third week of April when Lee suggested that Jackson unloose a major offensive to draw Union attention to the western district. Lee stated: "I have hoped in the present divided condition of the enemy's forces that a successful blow may be dealt them by a rapid combination of our troops before they can be strengthened themselves either in position or by re-enforcements."

Correspondence between the two generals from start to end of the ensuing Valley campaign fostered a mutual admiration. Lee basked in Jackson's accomplishments, for he saw in Jackson one of his own strong beliefs: the inferior side must always be daring and willing to fight when the opportunity presented itself.

Confederate army's chief of staff. Lee wrote his wife that he could not see either "advantage or pleasure" in the ignominious assignment. Yet he accepted the post without complaint but with the hope that it would lead in time to an assignment in the field.

Lee drew reinforcements to Virginia from all over the South. While he interfered little with the operations of the main army under Gen. Joseph E. Johnston, his friend since West Point days, he did superintend all other military activity in the state. That included perhaps Lee's most important task: containing Gen. George B. McClellan's massive Army of the Potomac advancing up the peninsula by keeping other Union forces in Virginia divided and away from the Richmond front.

He was successful in that endeavor. Yet the presidential adviser had to endure the frustration

Jackson was approaching the climax of the Valley fighting when Lee came to the forefront of Confederate command. On May 31, Johnston attacked a portion of McClellan's main Union army at Seven Pines, a hamlet only nine miles east of Richmond. Nightfall was bringing an end to the first day's struggle when Johnston fell seriously wounded. He was one of only two commanding officers to be wounded in action during the Civil War.

President Davis wasted no time in ordering Lee to enter the field and take charge of the Army of Northern Virginia. The survival of the unsteady Confederacy now rested with a man who had never led a military unit larger than a regiment. Moreover, Lee's unspectacular accomplishments to date were obscure to almost every-

one but President Davis. He was a desk soldier thrust into the front lines. To most Confederate soldiers in the field, the new commanding general was only a name.

No hesitation or indecision marked Lee's course. His courage and audacity were evident from the outset of his Civil War service. Lee had a quality of grandeur that resulted from a harmony of the powerful elements in his nature. A soldier of immense dignity, a gentleman who seldom indulged in levity, Lee was always the unruffled master of himself. His gentle nature and deep religious faith stood on a par with his determination as a general and his devotion to his southern birthright.

Lee masked his feelings with tremendous equipoise. He possessed what a friend called "a

Lee and Davis rode into a clearing where the June 30 fighting at Glendale had begun. The two were watching the action when up rode colorful Gen. A. P. Hill. "Little Powell" announced that both men were in his sector of responsibility, they were in danger, and they must withdraw at once. President and commander did as told. Seconds later, a shell exploded on the spot where they had been.

Citizens of Fredericksburg were huddling in anxiety when, on Thursday, November 20, 1862, Lee with Longstreet and the lead elements of the Confederate army rode into the town. The cheering was brief; residents had to abandon Fredericksburg for their own good. A major battle was imminent.

LEE'S SADDLE

imagine a Christian who was not a gentleman, or a gentleman who was not a Christian.

This product of Virginia aristocracy was noticeably thoughtful and considerate of the feelings of others. If a courier arrived at headquarters and looked hungry or fatigued, the commander ordered food or rest for the man before attending to the communiqué that he had received. Lee never raised his voice. He might be forced into an expression of anger, but when that occurred, he would without fail seek out the recipient later and offer profuse apologies. Only rarely did he express negative opinions about fellow officers. "General, your horse looks like it might be in need of exercise," was a gentle prod that told the recipient to give more attention to his duties. Further, lieutenants who expressed pessimistic outlooks in Lee's hearing quickly found themselves transferred elsewhere.

Apart from religion and family, all of Lee's thoughts were centered on the military. He did practically no general reading, nor did he ever accumulate a library of any consequence. Yet in strategy and tactics, in the preparation of earthworks and other aspects of field engineering, Lee made himself proficient by hard study. Nobody in America in the mid-nineteenth century knew military science quite as well as Lee.

His devotion to duty was absolute. Lee summarized it well when he told his youngest son: "Do your duty in all things. You cannot do more. You should never wish to do less."

Because Lee was who he was, men in the ranks viewed him from a distance and treated him with godlike respect. The affection that every one of Lee's soldiers possessed was hero worship. A Virginia infantryman, after seeing Lee for the first time, stated in a letter home: "It is impossible for me to describe the impression made upon me by his bearing and manners. I felt myself in the presence of a great man. . . . Every motion is instinct with natural grace, and yet there is dignity which . . . makes one feel a sense of confidence and trust that is delightful."

fierce and violent temper, prone to intense expression." Yet Lee was able to exercise "almost perfect control" over that temper. Finely balanced, with magnificent self-control, Lee commanded men through respect and wonder rather than through iron-willed discipline and fear. His leadership was paternal instead of autocratic.

The personal characteristics that he brought to the Civil War were an admirable mixture of moralist and militarist. Lee's gracious manners were a reflection of the deep and earnest faith he practiced. He read his Episcopal *Book of Common Prayer* daily; he reverently submitted himself to God's will with the devotion of a little child.

Once asked the secret of his generalship, Lee answered: "I think and work with all my power to bring the troops to the right place at the right time; then I have done my duty. As soon as I order them into battle, I leave my army in the hands of God." Lee's piety was so simple that it can be reduced to a basic maxim: he could never

As so often happened in the Civil War, rain followed the end of the fighting at Gettysburg. A disappointed Lee rode through the nighttime downpour with Longstreet. To a British observer, he remarked, "This has been a sad day for us, Colonel—a sad day." Then Lee drew straight in the saddle and added, "But we can't always expect to gain victories."

The secrets of Lee's military success would emerge clearly during the three years he commanded the principal weapon for the defense of Richmond: the Army of Northern Virginia. First, war was a passion with Lee. Brilliant as an engineer, unexcelled in the use of inner lines of defense as well as field fortifications, he found himself committed by Confederate policy to a defensive posture. Yet Lee went beyond a static, unmovable stance. To him, defense was fluid and active—something designed to prevent the enemy's concentration and to take away his initiative at critical moments.

Audacity became his byword. He was a general, Douglas Southall Freeman observed, "born to make the attack." To most observers, Lee was too quiet and reserved to be aggressive. However, he was always thinking in terms of offense. His idea of parrying a blow was to beat his opponent to the punch and strike a blow of his own. Lee was the first of the Confederate field commanders in the eastern theater to employ strategy in defense and to pick points for battle.

Even though a hard-hitting and relentless field commander, Lee was also a merciful man sensitively aware of the suffering that warfare imposes. During the Mexican War, he told his wife: "You have no idea what a horrible sight a battlefield is." At the height of one of his most smashing Civil War victories, Lee observed that war might be fascinating if it were not so horrible.

Good physical vitality would bless Lee's efforts only through the first half of the Civil War. In 1861 Lee was a picture of near-perfect health. He had been seriously ill but once in his life. Yet despite his great powers of endurance, the Civil War broke Lee. A number of maladies struck him during the last half of the war. His physical condition deteriorated on a parallel course with the fortunes of the Confederacy.

Lee was an extremely perceptive man. He could discern an officer's strengths and weaknesses in an instant. A familiarity with many of the opposing generals whom he faced enabled Lee to capitalize on that understanding of human nature. In contrast, Union commanders sent to fight Lee never quite seemed to gain an accurate picture of the man, his thoughts, or his abilities.

Morale is always a good test of generalship. Instilling high spirits in an army that never had sufficient quantities of essential stores and clothing was one of Lee's greatest achievements. He led with reliance on unshakable morale, and it worked all the way to the end. Lee would become so confident of his soldiers that by 1863 he thought his army invincible. Because that army was so well led, the men came to the same conclusion.

Fredericksburg was Lee's easiest victory. A dozen times Union forces assaulted the Confederate lines. A dozen times they were repulsed. Atop the high ground, Lee turned to Longstreet. "It is well that war is so terrible!" he exclaimed. "We should grow too fond of it!"

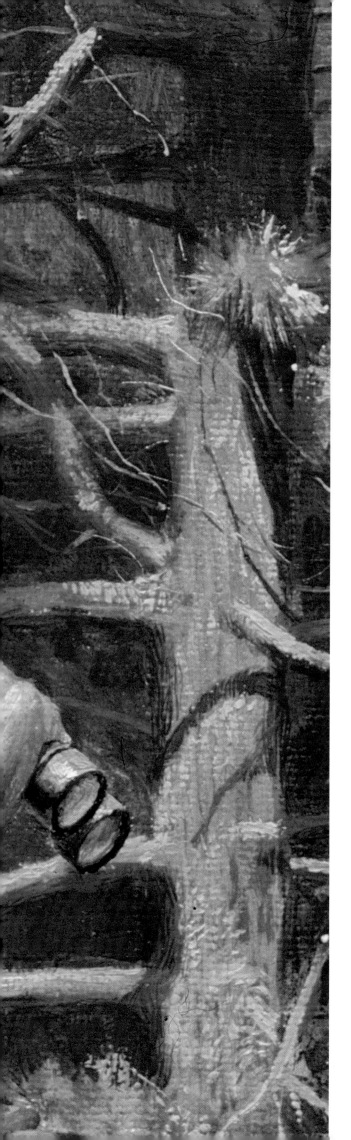

PART

Virginia Orphan

VIRGINIA ORPHAN

FEW GREAT MILITARY LEADERS have ever emerged from more humble beginnings. His childhood was so steeped in sadness that he would not discuss that period of his life.

Thomas Jackson was born in January 1824 at Clarksburg in the mountains of northwest Virginia. His father was a ne'er-do-well attorney given more to business speculation and gambling than to preserving the luster of the family name. Both parents died before Jackson reached the age of seven. Separated almost completely from his brother and sister, the withdrawn and lonely youth spent his boyhood years on the Lewis County farm of a bachelor uncle. In that environment, Jackson received basic security rather than fatherly love.

Although having only the rudiments of an education, Jackson in 1842 secured an appointment to the U.S. Military Academy. (He gained admission only because the first appointee from Jackson's congressional district quit West Point after only a day.) For Jackson, West Point was the one opportunity in his life for advancement. He was painfully aware of his poor scholastic preparation, his physical awkwardness, his lack of social graces. Hence, the introspective mountain boy developed impassivity as a protection while he concentrated all of his energies on the single purpose of acquiring an education.

Such a pursuit of learning was necessary. Jackson survived the first year "by the skin of my teeth," he declared. Studies consumed his waking hours, for every subject was new and difficult. An artillery professor remembered Cadet Jackson as "raw boned, stiff jointed, and totally devoid of all grace and motion." When ordered to execute the manual of loading a cannon, Jackson "would go all to pieces." Perspiration would drip over an expression of "sorrow & suffering," continuing until the cadet eventually performed the drill correctly.

Academy friendships were few during those four years. Jackson's only confidante was his married sister, Laura, to whom he clung by letter with an almost desperate bond. By sheer determination and unbroken diligence—both embodied in one of his favorite axioms, "You may be whatever you resolve to be"—he graduated seventeenth of fifty-nine cadets in his class. Some of his professors remarked that if the curriculum had extended over another year, the persistent Jackson would have ranked number one in the 1846 class that included such future generals as George B. McClellan, Jesse Reno, Darius N. Couch, Truman Seymour, George Stoneman, Cadmus M. Wilcox, and George E. Pickett.

High academic standing brought Jackson appointment to the artillery, the branch of service that was always his first military love. The Mexican War reached out at once for the young lieutenant. Jackson took full advantage of the opportunity. Gallantry in action at Veracruz, Contreras, and Chapultepec earned Jackson three brevet promotions to the rank of major. Even army commander Winfield Scott praised him publicly. Jackson had served in the field only six months, but he had outperformed every other member of his West Point class.

He gained invaluable lessons from the war. The transition from book knowledge to practical application is a challenge to every soldier, and Jackson did well. He learned about handling volunteer soldiers, how to stand firm in battle, and the extent to which discipline is fundamental to good soldier life. From a tactical standpoint, Jackson learned the advantage of flanking movements.

AT LEFT:

History knows him as "Stonewall." VMI cadets dubbed him "Tom Fool." Some men not imbued with his deep faith referred to him as "Old Blue Light." But to his soldiers, he was first to last affectionately called "Old Jack."

OVERLEAF:

Jackson's "inner family" became one of the strongest staffs in the Civil War. It included, left to right, Surgeon Hunter McGuire, Adjutant "Sandie" Pendleton, Quartermaster John A. Harman, aide James Power Smith, and mapmaker "Jed" Hotchkiss. Jackson required all of his staff to be devout, dutiful, and early risers.

In 1851 Jackson left the army to become a professor of physics and artillery tactics at the Virginia Military Institute in Lexington. There his adult education began. He knew painfully little about social conduct. The art of conversation was beyond Jackson; *romance* was a word he could not define; religion was just becoming a powerful interest.

Then there were the idiosyncrasies. Jackson's mannerisms were stiff and unorthodox. He became convinced that every one of his major organs was malfunctioning. To control the pangs of dyspepsia, the Virginian adhered to a strict diet. He once told an astonished hostess: "The moment a grain of black pepper touches my tongue, I lose all strength in my right leg." For his other ailments, Jackson relied on water treatments at spas throughout the East.

Meanwhile, and during the fourth of his life that he spent at VMI, he was a teacher known more for dullness and peculiarities than for inspiring knowledge. Ineffectiveness in class and sternness in all faculty duties made Jackson unpopular with most of the institute's student body. "He is undoubtedly the worst teacher that God ever made," one youngster asserted. Cadets played pranks on him and referred to him by such nicknames as "Tom Fool." An upperclassman once wrote: "Great lord almighty, what a wonder! Major Jackson: Hell & thunder!"

A new Jackson evolved in other ways that decade. He painfully learned the rudiments of social mixing. In 1853 he married Elinor Junkin, daughter of a Lexington Presbyterian minister and college president. "Ellie" died a year later in childbirth, as did the son she was carrying.

The one thing that sustained Jackson in this tragedy was his faith. In the autumn of his first year at VMI, after a long search for a comfortable

In an age when the average male was 5 feet, 7 inches tall and weighed 135 pounds, Jackson was unusually large. He stood just under 6 feet and weighed 170 pounds. His eyes were sky blue, his hair brown. Large hands and enormous feet made his rather high-pitched voice seem odd.

denomination, Jackson became a member of the Presbyterian Church. Quickly he developed into a leading Calvinist of his age. Jackson announced to one and all that he would never "violate the known will of God." He never did.

One of Jackson's closest prewar friends exclaimed: "Never have I known a holier man. Never have I seen a human being as thoroughly governed by duty. He lived only to please God; his daily life was a daily offering up of himself." Moses D. Hoge, a prominent Richmond cleric, observed after the Civil War: "To attempt to portray the life of Jackson while leaving out the religious element would be like undertaking to portray Switzerland without making mention of the Alps."

Jackson attended every church service he could. Believing that salvation lay in prayer, he offered thanks to God whenever he drank a glass of water, opened a letter, or walked into class. In 1852 he organized a young men's Bible class in Lexington; three years later, he established and began teaching a black Sunday school class in open defiance of a Virginia law that forbade teaching slaves to read and write.

His 1857 marriage to Mary Anna Morrison, also a Presbyterian minister's daughter, would last less than six years but bring him the most prolonged happiness he ever knew. Five slaves lived at the Jackson home. Jackson's views on the institution were typically simple. Human bondage was something established by the Almighty for reasons man could not be expected to know. As Jackson viewed his responsibilities, he was to introduce the servants to all the promises of Christianity and to treat them with fatherlike attachment. That affection was genuine, and it was reciprocated in full.

VMI cadets still made jokes about "the Major": his absent-mindedness, boring lectures, lack of humor, abnormally long walking strides, total adherence to detail and discipline. Yet his life at the institute could be compared to a dull flint. When opportunity struck the spark, the marvel of genius would explode.

Following abolitionist John Brown's 1859 raid into Virginia and the rumbling across the nation as war clouds gathered, Jackson the proven

One of the dramatic moments in VMI history came when Maj. Thomas J. Jackson led the corps of cadets to war. The clock atop the barracks had just tolled the half-hour when Jackson gave the command to march. Behind him was faculty colleague Raleigh E. Colston. The institute flag waved above the head of the column of two as it started down the hill en route to Richmond.

soldier and Mexican War hero became more respected in the upper region of Virginia's Shenandoah Valley.

The Old Dominion left the Union in April 1861, and Jackson dutifully followed the path of his beloved state. Doing so brought instant personal loss. His sister, Laura, was a Union activist in the northwestern part of the state. A lifetime of shared love and unbroken correspondence came to an end. Now every member of Jackson's immediate family was gone.

He took a contingent of VMI cadets to Richmond to serve as drillmasters for the thousands of army recruits gathering at what became the capital of both a state and the Confederate States of America. Jackson never saw Lexington again. By then he was thirty-seven. He stood just under six feet in height and weighed near 170 pounds. His high-pitched voice did not fit his heavy size. Dark blue eyes, pointed nose, brown hair and beard, a high forehead, and the thin lips of a zealot marked his facial features. His hands were unusually large, his feet enormous.

Oblivious to dress in the first months of the Civil War, he was recognizable by his seediness. Jackson even sat a horse awkwardly, body bent far forward as if he were leaning into a stiff wind. He was known more for his silence than for any utterances. In short, Jackson gave no appearance of ability, much less of genius.

It had been fourteen years since he had last seen combat. Yet Jackson swept into civil war with cool professionalism and abiding faith in God's presence. He saw divine intercession in the breakup of the Union. God had levied a curse on the land. Victory would come to the side that most feared the Lord. The relentless pursuit of victory was the relentless pursuit of faith.

His first assignment as a colonel of Virginia volunteers was command of Harpers Ferry, the

As a young boy in the mountains of northwestern Virginia, Jackson rode horses in local races. He early adopted the jockey's posture of leaning forward over the horse's mane. Years later, General Jackson appeared awkward in the saddle, yet he was such a stable horseman that he often napped while in the saddle.

northernmost point of the Confederacy. There the Potomac and Shenandoah Rivers cut through mountainous country and come together. Harpers Ferry boasted one of the nation's largest armories; the vital Baltimore and Ohio Railroad crossed the Potomac there on a nine-hundred-foot bridge; the heavily traveled Chesapeake and Ohio Canal hugged the northern bank of the Potomac in that region; from Harpers Ferry southward, both roads and railroad led into the agriculturally and strategically rich Shenandoah Valley.

Some twenty-five hundred poorly equipped and totally inexperienced volunteers had assembled at Harpers Ferry. Jackson threw all personal liberties to the wind as he trained and molded recruits into soldiers. Drill and discipline became his bywords. "Jackson is considered rigid to the point of tyranny," stated one young soldier, who then expressed surprise on learning that the colonel was a deeply pious man.

In July 1861 Jackson received promotion to brigadier general and command of Virginia's First Brigade. He was leading infantry for the first time in his career. His five regiments were all from the Valley of Virginia. Under Jackson's strong but paternal guidance, the regiments developed pride before experience—a bond before bloodshed— that would make them one of the most famous fighting units in American military history.

Fame came early to Jackson in the Civil War, but in typical fashion he stated that any glory was due "to God alone." On July 21 the first major land battle of the war occurred in northern Virginia at Manassas Junction, near Bull Run. By afternoon Union assaults were on the verge of shattering Jackson's position on the left of the Confederate line. The brigadier and his thirty-five hundred men calmly blunted a Federal attack by making a "stonewall" defense on a commanding plateau. Despite a broken finger from a bullet wound, Jackson waited for the proper moment and then unleashed an attack of his own. It was the first step in a victorious Southern counterstroke.

Thereafter, he was Stonewall Jackson and his men the Stonewall Brigade. The sobriquet was a

The first major battle of the Civil War occurred near Manassas and Bull Run, Virginia. Jackson, clad in the blue uniform of a VMI professor, calmly stabilized his inexperienced soldiers atop the key ridge on the field. A nickname and lasting fame were about to come to the general and his men.

misnomer, for Jackson's genius and accomplishments lay in powerful offensive strikes rather than rocklike defensive stands. "Stonewall" became the name by which the press and the public knew Jackson. To his men, however, he was always and affectionately "Old Jack."

Promotion to major general came in the autumn, and with it command of the 165-mile-long Shenandoah Valley formed by the two most eastern ranges of the Allegheny Mountains. Jackson wasted no time in making his presence felt to friend as well as foe. He consolidated small, scattered commands into one force, substituted discipline for disarray, converted fun-loving recruits into serious-minded soldiers, and introduced war into the Valley on an unforgettable scale.

In the first frigid days of January 1862, Jackson led his little army on a campaign. Less than fifty miles away, Union troops held the towns of Bath, Hancock, and Romney. This put the fertile and strategic valley of the South Branch of the Potomac River under enemy occupation. If Jackson could occupy the region, all of the northwestern part of the state might come into the Confederate fold.

Southern soldiers fought snow, ice, exposure, and Yankees, but succeeded in occupying Romney. When Confederate Secretary of War Judah P. Benjamin thoughtlessly directed Jackson to abandon the place two weeks later, Jackson did so—and resigned from the army. He could not operate as a departmental commander in the face of uninformed civilian interference almost two hundred miles away in Richmond. A host of admirers, beginning with Virginia governor John Letcher, persuaded the general to withdraw his resignation.

Jackson's problems remained twofold. He had to keep the Federals from occupying the

On November 4, 1861, newly promoted Major General Jackson said farewell to his Stonewall Brigade as he departed to take command of Confederate defenses in the Shenandoah Valley. Jackson delivered a moving speech to the soldiers, then galloped away to echoes of the Rebel Yell. He would later term the peculiar Confederate battle cry "the sweetest music I have ever heard."

Shenandoah Valley (which provided so much foodstuffs to the Southern armies that it was called the breadbasket of the Confederacy). Jackson's other task was to prevent enemy forces in the western part of Virginia from reinforcing Gen. George B. McClellan and his army as it advanced on Richmond. To fulfill those assignments, Jackson had six thousand troops. Opposing him were thirty-eight thousand Federals. The Confederate leader was undeterred. "If the Valley is lost," Jackson stated, "Virginia is lost."

Thus, in the spring of 1862 he undertook a series of movements designed to fulfill both of his military responsibilities. Jackson was a comparative unknown at the outset. Three months later he was arguably the best-known field commander in the world.

The Valley campaign began with a March 23 Confederate attack at Kernstown in the northern end of the Shenandoah. Jackson quickly found himself the victim of faulty reconnaissance. Instead of encountering only the rear guard of the Union army, as expected, he came face to face with a full division of the enemy. The Confederates suffered a tactical setback at Kernstown, but Jackson gained a strategic victory by forcing Union authorities to withhold reinforcements from leaving the area and joining McClellan.

Jackson then utilized the ingredients that made him famous: secret movements, hard marches, knowledge of terrain, unexpected tactics, heavy assaults concentrated at one point, and singleness of purpose. This strange, complex, and lonely Presbyterian who rode silently at the head of his troops crisscrossed the Valley in ways that kept his opponents totally off balance. Jackson first appeared in the mountains west of the Valley and defeated a Federal advance at the hamlet of McDowell. Jackson then retraced his steps back into the Shenandoah. There he linked up with Gen. Richard S. Ewell's division and staged a rapid, secret advance all the way to the northern end of the Valley.

On May 23, Confederates overwhelmed a stunned Union garrison at Front Royal. Two days

The closest friend Jackson ever had was his second wife, Anna. During the winter of 1861–62, they were together at Winchester, Virginia. Anna often came to see him at his headquarters in the Moore home. When they parted on the eve of the Valley campaign, Anna was pregnant.

later, Jackson's men routed the main Federal force at Winchester. One of the most exhilarating moments in Jackson's career came when he rode among his troops advancing through the streets of Winchester to the cheers and joyful sobs of hundreds of liberated townspeople.

Union efforts subsequently got underway to trap Jackson in the lower (northern) part of the Shenandoah Valley. Two Federal armies moved from opposite directions like a closing vise behind the Confederates. Yet Jackson's "foot cavalry," as the infantrymen styled themselves because of their marching ability, tramped through rain and mud more quickly than the enemy hosts could move against them. Jackson escaped the "slamming door" and retired up the Valley.

The separate forces of Federal Gens. John C. Frémont and James Shields gave chase. On June 8, Jackson turned at Cross Keys with part of his little army and stunned Frémont with a heavy attack. The following day, Jackson assaulted Shields four miles to the east at Port Republic. A hard-fought victory came at noon. Jackson withdrew his army to a convenient gap in the Blue Ridge Mountains. From there he could assail the flank of any Federal army that tried again to move southward up the Valley. Then he wrote Lee of what he had accomplished and asked what Lee next wished him to do.

At times Jackson had seemed hopelessly outnumbered. His soldiers had suffered continually from lack of food, clothing, and other essentials. Yet in forty-eight days they had marched 646 miles, fought four battles, six skirmishes, and a dozen delaying actions. By mid-June, three Federal armies were in retreat.

Old Jack was the man of the hour in the Southern nation. Through unsurpassed boldness he had achieved the most spectacular Confederate success of the war up to that point. The little-known former professor had saved Richmond from quick capture, disrupted all Federal plans for operations in Virginia, and defeated three separate enemy armies that together outnumbered him four-to-one. In addition, he had ensured the

Sunday, May 25, 1862: Jackson's "foot cavalry" routed the Union army from Winchester and entered the town in triumph. The general wrote his wife the following day, "The people seemed nearly frantic with joy. . . . Our entrance into Winchester was one of the most stirring scenes of my life."

safety of the Valley, inflicted seven thousand casualties at a cost of fewer than half that number, seized nine thousand small arms, and confiscated tons of badly needed arms and stores.

Gen. Richard S. Ewell, his second-in-command, was asked at the end of the Valley campaign to evaluate Jackson's performance. The usually crusty Ewell responded: "Well, sir, when he commenced it I thought him crazy; before he ended it I thought him inspired."

Jackson *was* inspired. In a note to his wife at the end of the campaign, he wrote: "God has been our shield, and to His name be all the glory." This was a fitting declaration, for by the conclusion of the three-month contest in the Shenandoah, Jackson's men were convinced that their general was in direct communication with heaven. He marched them until their legs had no feeling, he drove them beyond exhaustion, he showed nothing but contempt for those who straggled or fell ill.

When the soldiers reached the field of battle, spitting cotton and stumbling from fatigue, Jackson flung them into combat and never gave thought to casualties until he had exploited every chance for gain. Credit for all accomplishments went to God. All the men got for their fighting and bravery and suffering was victory after victory. But that was enough. They were Jackson's foot cavalry: unmatched for speed on the march and a proven fighting force a cut above other volunteers in that civil war between citizen-soldiers.

A cavalry officer who served briefly as an aide on Jackson's staff painted an intriguing word picture of the general: "He is ever monosyllabic and receives and delivers a message as if the bearer was a conduct pipe from one ear to another. There is a magnetism in Jackson, but it is not personal. All admire his genius and great deeds; no one could love the man for himself. He seems to be cut off from his fellow men and to commune with his own spirit only, or with spirits of which we know not. . . . Whenever he moves about on his old sorrel, with faded uniform and weather-stained cap slouched down over his left eye, and one shoulder some two inches higher than the other, most men shout with enthusiasm. . . . It is a saying in the army if a shout is heard, 'There goes Jackson or a rabbit!'"

He had three cardinal rules in battle: mystify your opponent, maneuver your men until you can throw your main force against a weak spot in the enemy's line, and be utterly ruthless in pursuit of the wounded foe. Jackson was harsh, for he hated weakness in any form. He exacted the last ounce of effort from his soldiers because he willingly gave every ounce of his own strength to the cause.

Nothing gave Jackson the appearance of a great conqueror. Wearing the dingy blue uniform of an "old" army officer and a VMI kepi that usually was pulled down on the bridge of his nose, Jackson rode to battle on his small horse with an abstracted air of concentration. Childhood hardships had made him so self-reliant that he rarely sought advice, civil or military. He talked no more than was necessary and took no one into his confidence except God—to whom he offered prayers several times each day—and his beloved wife, Anna, who was then carrying his child.

That Jackson had been able to undertake his daring campaign in the Valley was the result of confidence in him by Gen. Robert E. Lee who, as military adviser to President Jefferson Davis, approved and oversaw Jackson's operations. A mutual understanding and respect between the two generals existed months before they merged their talents into a common undertaking.

By the time Jackson completed his movements and secured the Shenandoah Valley, Lee was in command of the Army of Northern Virginia. The safety of Richmond lay squarely on his shoulders. Lee considered sending Jackson back down the Valley to occupy the northern end. Jackson loved the Shenandoah but was not in favor of such a move, he said, "until we are in a condition under the blessing of Providence to hold the country."

Lee responded with a letter to President Davis: "I think the sooner Jackson can move this way, the better—the first object now is to defeat McClellan." With that, Lee summoned Jackson and his Valley force for a concentrated attack against the major Union army. Jackson's columns promptly snaked over the Blue Ridge Mountains and marched through the rolling piedmont country toward their capital.

His attitude toward the Civil War by then was embedded deep in his being. He was defending his homeland, of course, but for Jackson the meaning of the war was more profound. God had placed a great curse on America for reasons no man could explain. The contest must be waged with total commitment because the most righteous side, in the eyes of the Almighty, would be triumphant.

Jackson's fervent prayer was that he might lead "an army of the living God as well as of its country." This burning devotion colored his whole outlook on the war. It turned him steel-cold, even merciless, at times. His favorite biblical passage was: "And we know that all things work together for good to them that love God, to them who are the called according to His purpose."

Jackson converted that Pauline saying into a military philosophy. Throughout this conflict between the pious and the Philistines, he would pursue New Testament faith with Old Testament fury.

Of the four horses Jackson had in the war, Little Sorrel was his favorite. He purchased the undersized mount as a gift for his wife, but horse and rider took an instant liking for each other. Little Sorrel died in 1886 at the age of thirty-five. The animal's stuffed remains are in the VMI Museum.

PART

III

Model Partnership

MODEL PARTNERSHIP

LEE TOOK COMMAND OF THE Army of Northern Virginia on June 1, 1862, in an atmosphere of doom. The Union army was only a half-day's march from Richmond. In the Confederate ranks, a professional soldier who had never led men in combat now commanded the South's foremost army. That force was indifferently organized, a crude and makeshift aggregation compared to the Union fighting machine in its front, and Confederate troops were spread haphazardly over an area larger than the city they were duty-bound to defend.

Inside Richmond was near chaos. Boxes and crates were being hauled to waiting trains. Town residents, government workers, even the Confederate Congress were fleeing the city. President Jefferson Davis had sent his family to North Carolina for safety. In the field, the new army chief was an unknown quantity. Resources and manpower were so limited that it seemed impossible to halt the Union tide slowly rolling forward from the east.

Not everyone despaired. A young officer in the capital told a friend early that month: "If there is one man in either army . . . head and shoulders above every other in audacity, it is General Lee! His name might be audacity. He will take more desperate chances and take them

Morale was always high in the Army of Northern Virginia because the men were well led and they knew it. At their head was Lee—godlike to untold numbers of soldiers. Jackson was the slasher—the attacker who fought with the savagery of an Old Testament warrior. Longstreet became the anchor—careful, reliable, and as solid as his huge physique.

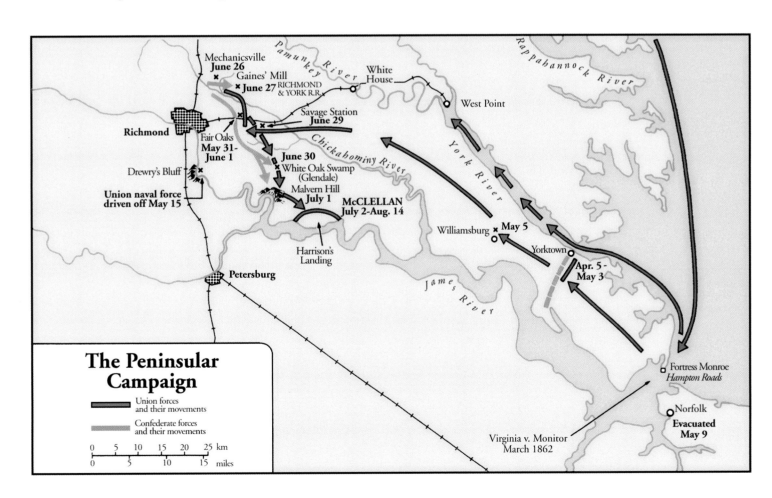

Picturesque James Ewell Brown "Jeb" Stuart (1833–64) would have romanticized any war. He rode hard and fought hard. Stuart had a compulsive desire for the limelight, but he possessed the right combination of daring and skill to achieve it repeatedly. Jackson, never given to compliments, termed Stuart "prompt, vigilant, and fearless."

McClellan. The defense he would wage was to be a heavy counteroffensive. What Lee was bringing to the Southern effort in Virginia was a grand strategy, the first introduced by the Confederates in their defense. In the final days of spring, Lee carefully nurtured an army hurting in numbers and morale. He raised spirits by his own inspiration; he shaped units to his own perceptions.

Among Lee's first strategic acts was to send his cavalry chief on a mission to ascertain where McClellan's right (or northern) flank ended. Twenty-nine-year-old Jeb Stuart was a good-looking, dashing, sometimes flamboyant general. He possessed all the instincts of a true cavalryman, good and bad. While Stuart could plunge deep into enemy-held territory and pull great feats with his troopers, he could not resist a bold stroke when a more careful move was in order. He demonstrated this at the outset of his association with Lee.

With 1,200 horsemen, Stuart embarked on his reconnaissance in customary fashion. The Confederates obtained the necessary information; then, in what Stuart considered a lark, the large cavalry force rode completely around the Union army and returned to Lee with 165 prisoners, 260 horses, and valuable information—all gained at a cost of one fatality. The "Ride Around McClellan" was a showy gesture, childish in conception but marvelous in results. It could not have come at a better time for sagging spirits in the South.

Lee rapidly made plans to abandon a static defense in favor of a more promising offense. As he studied maps of the peninsula where the enemy stood massed, one feature of the area kept drawing his attention. The Chickahominy was not really a river, as the charts stated. It was a flowing swamp. How deep it was and how wide it ran depended on when last it rained. By early June 1862 the stream was a swollen bog that meandered diagonally across the Virginia Peninsula as it made its way southeastward to the James River.

Innocent in appearance, the swampland had become a military hazard for the Union army.

quicker than any other general in this country, North or South; and you will live to see it, too."

Hesitation was not a part of Lee's makeup. So much needed to be learned in those first days of June, but in Lee's estimation so much more needed to be done. His experience in field operations was limited to staff work in the Mexican War. He was unfamiliar with many problems as well as many untested officers inside the army he now found himself commanding. Lee also knew that Federal Gen. George B. McClellan's forces threatening Richmond were more powerful in every respect than anything Lee could place in his front. Only total defeat in battle could stop "those people," Lee contended. He must strike for victory, and do it quickly. Time was another enemy.

The firm idea in Lee's mind from the beginning was to halt the long retreats up the peninsula. Lee intended to seize the initiative from

[58]

The Chickahominy sliced through the line of McClellan's 105,000 men. Most of the Federals were on the south side of the swamp, near Richmond. A lone corps stood on the north bank. It waited hopefully for 40,000 reinforcements to come down from Fredericksburg to help end the Civil War with a massive, two-front assault on the Confederate capital.

McClellan was deliberate, careful, and cautious. Almost daily he begged for reinforcements. Abraham Lincoln, his patience sorely tried, once exclaimed: "If I gave General McClellan all the troops he wanted, they would not have room [on the peninsula] to lie down. They would have to sleep standing up."

Meanwhile, the vastly superior Federal army pursued the safest possible course. In his chess game of war, McClellan intended to edge forward toward Richmond by slow stages, fortifying the country as he moved, carefully rolling up his heavy artillery until the guns could blast a hole in the Southern defenses and open the door to checkmate: the capture of the enemy's capital.

Lee was quite aware of what McClellan was doing. How to stop it was both the problem and the challenge. His solution was as bold a plan as a general under the circumstances could make. Outnumbered two-to-one, with the largest army the Western Hemisphere had ever seen cautiously moving toward Richmond and another enemy force equal in size to Lee's defenders ready to strike from the north, Lee determined to attack first.

McClellan always believed that the enemy had more troops than he did. Lee would exploit that weakness by leaving a small but highly demonstrative screen in McClellan's front to hold the Union army in place. Then the bulk of Lee's Army of Northern Virginia would slip to the north and assail McClellan's separated force north of the Chickahominy. Stonewall Jackson was bringing his army down from the Shenandoah Valley and would turn the Federal flank that Lee's men had battered. If successful, this two-edged counteroffensive would send the much-heralded

Federal army tumbling south like a line of erect dominoes collapsing in turn.

Few generals have ever taken a larger risk. Lee was going to gamble the independence of the Southern Confederacy by tricky maneuvers. He would divide his numerically inferior army in the presence of the enemy. Further, he was leaving three poised Federal armies in northern Virginia with nothing holding them back but apprehension over the name "Jackson." And Lee all the while would be attacking rather than maximizing his small army's strength behind earthworks.

The strategy seemed blatantly reckless. Yet Lee had known McClellan in the prewar years. The gifted young militarist (he, like Lee, had graduated second in his West Point class) had intellect, energy, and tremendous charisma. He thrived on Napoleonic poses and maximum press coverage. What he lacked as a soldier was that

The handsome George B. McClellan (1826–85) was a brilliant organizer who shaped the Army of the Potomac into the grandest fighting machine ever seen in America. However, beneath a messianic complex and bubbly optimism lay the procrastination of a perfectionist, gnawing self-doubts, and a reluctance to do battle.

They were the two most famous and familiar figures in the Confederacy. Yet Southern troops reacted differently at the sight of Jackson and Lee. "When General Lee rides by, the soldiers gaze at him in silent admiration," a young lieutenant wrote in the autumn of 1862. "But whenever Jackson is seen, every soldier's mouth flies wide open" with cheers.

The largest and costliest of the Seven Days battles near Richmond was Gaines' Mill. Lee's first victory came when the Texas Brigade broke the Federal line but incurred great losses in the process. The next morning, Jackson and Lee surveyed the ground where the Confederates had charged. Jackson exclaimed, "The men who carried this position were soldiers indeed!"

cold, instinctive fondness for battle present in all successful field commanders.

Lee possessed that ingredient fully. He saw it as the only thing on which the Confederate experiment could depend for victory. By taking control of events away from McClellan, Lee would then be laying down all of the ground rules in the campaign. That would weigh heavily in counterbalancing the disparity of numbers between the armies of North and South. All of these points Lee outlined in a June 23 meeting with his principal generals at his Richmond field headquarters. Jackson, already fatigued by two months of hard operations in the Valley, rode the better part of two consecutive days and nights to attend the afternoon conference. No one knew at the time that the stern, reticent, seemingly tireless general was at the limit of his physical and mental endurance. Never robust, as needful of sleep as any man, Jackson was only a day or so away from collapse.

On June 26, the Confederate attack began. This was the first offensive of the war by the South's premier army. Movements and execution had all of the attributes of a shakedown cruise. Everything went awry. Only Lee's audacity remained consistent. His battle plan proved too sophisticated for that early stage of the Civil War. Bold strategy succumbed to sloppy tactics. Coordination never existed. Orders were infrequent and generally inaccurate with respect to terrain and enemy positions. The fighting devolved into unconnected melees as if each of Lee's division commanders had been left alone to do combat where and as best he could. Stonewall Jackson's performance seemed the greatest disappointment of all.

The Seven Days battles began with the greater part of Lee's army crossing the Chickahominy, driving Federal pickets from the village of Mechanicsville, and assaulting the main enemy position on high ground behind Beaver Dam Creek. In command of the Union lines there was Gen. Fitz John Porter, a handsome, careful man who fought well when curbing his ambition and a tendency to gossip. Lee's advance was premature;

Jackson's men were nowhere in sight. The Federals blew gaping holes in the assaulting columns. It was fortunate for Lee's army that darkness brought an end to the four-hour, hopelessly one-sided contest.

Now at last McClellan realized that the Confederate army was far north on his flank. A quick advance straight ahead, and Richmond could be his. Unfortunately for the Union, McClellan did not operate that way. He promptly assumed the defensive, abandoned his supply line with the York River, and turned south to establish a new base on the James.

During the night, with no reinforcements at hand, Porter withdrew his Federals five miles eastward to a crescent-shaped position on high ground at Gaines' Mill. Lee renewed the attacks at dawn the next morning. Jackson's army was expected momentarily to slam into Porter's flank. Hours of combat transpired, casualties mounted, and Jackson—led down the wrong road by a guide—continued to be hours late.

Anxieties mounted among the army's high command. A couple of hours before nightfall, Jackson galloped onto the field. The army commander greeted his lieutenant with obvious relief. Jackson mumbled something in reply and issued quick orders for his divisions to fan out into battle formation. The sun was dipping toward the western horizon when the full Confederate army, some fifty-five thousand men, began the largest assault of the war to date. Soldiers struck through swamps and underbrush before rushing uphill against the strongly defended Union position.

Lee was determined to break the enemy line. His troops did their best. Wave after wave went forward; cannon fire and musketry were deafening; dead and dying soldiers sprawled everywhere. Confederate pressure finally became too much. Porter's line broke, Union guns were abandoned, some blueclad regiments were surrounded and captured in their fieldworks. Lee now controlled all of the peninsula north of the Chickahominy. The Union army, McClellan's reference to a "strategic withdrawal" notwithstanding, was in full retreat southward.

AT RIGHT:

Lee, Longstreet, Stuart, and Jackson are concluding their August 24, 1862, conference on how to stop the advance of Federal forces under Gen. John Pope. Jackson and half of the outnumbered Southern army would make a circuitous march to get behind Pope and possibly destroy the Union supply depot. As Lee stood to wish Jackson well, his lieutenant said, "I will be moving within the hour."

OVERLEAF:

With plumed hat, flashy uniform, and flair for the dramatic, Jeb Stuart seemed an incarnation from the age of cavaliers. His ride around the entire Union army in June 1862 raised the question (one Southern newspaper chortled) "of whether the annals of warfare furnish so daring a deed."

He was the senior corps commander in the Army of Northern Virginia—a huge man with accompanying strong-mindedness. Lee relied heavily on James Longstreet (1821– 1904). Yet "Old Pete" proved to have off-setting qualities: patriotic but petulant, aggressive but ambitious, self-confident but at times self-righteous.

Tons of Union supplies were cast aside or burned, field hospitals and their occupants were left to the mercy of advancing Confederates as the Union army sought safety under the heavy guns of naval vessels anchored in the James. Lee pushed hard with the hope that he could strike a crippling blow to McClellan's army while it was on the move. However, after each clash, Federals left the battlefield and took a new position. In none of the contests was Lee able to get his entire army into action at the same moment. His men fought gallantly; they simply were not strong enough to deliver the punch necessary to destroy the Union army.

A sharp but indecisive engagement occurred on June 29 at Savage Station. Early the next morning, Lee and Jackson held a brief confer-ence. Jackson's only orders were to press the Fed-erals southward. He did so as far as White Oak

Swamp, where a full Union corps blocked the way. Still operating under Lee's outdated June 29 directive to guard the Chickahominy crossings behind him, Jackson spent the afternoon a vic-tim of utter fatigue. He slept while Confederates and Federals fought to a stalemate a few miles away at Glendale. Again Lee had almost brought McClellan to bay.

The climax came July 1 at Malvern Hill, a broad elevation over which the road to McClellan's new supply base at Harrison's Landing passed. Malvern Hill was the last natural defense for the Union army before reaching the James. McClellan positioned long rows of cannon hub to hub along the brow of the high ground. Heavy siege guns were behind the field pieces. Union infantry filled in all of the nooks and crevices.

Lee, still driving hard, should have given more thought to the obstacles atop Malvern Hill. Yet he was convinced from the large amount of discarded Federal equipment that McClellan was greatly weakened. One more concerted attack might bring triumph.

Fatigue, poor roads, imprecise orders, and undue haste all played a role in dooming the Confederate onslaught at Malvern Hill. However, the main impediment to Lee's hopes was the strength of the Union position. With a clear field of fire, the Federals participated in what could be likened to a horrible turkey shoot. Whenever a Confederate battery dared to move into firing position, fifty or more Union cannon blew it apart. McClellan's guns raked the lines of advanc-ing Confederate infantry unmercifully. "It was not war," one of Lee's division commanders noted, "it was murder."

The Seven Days ended, so did the Peninsular campaign, and everything came to a close on a strange note. McClellan won all of the battles save one (Gaines' Mill). His army lost 10 percent of its manpower, fifty-two cannon, and thirty-one thousand small arms. A fourth of Lee's army fell, including ten thousand soldiers gone for good. Over the long haul, the Confederacy could not afford such victories. "Our success has not been as great or as complete as I could have desired," Lee confessed to his wife.

His accomplishments had come in the wake of battle losses at Roanoke Island, Pea Ridge, and Shiloh, plus the loss of New Orleans and the mouth of the Mississippi River. Despite all the mistakes and lost opportunities in the Seven Days east of Richmond, the offensive baptism for the Confederate army was a success. True, Lee had failed to destroy the Union army. His losses had been stunning. Yet he emerged a hero. The Southern people saw the victory but did not count the cost. Lee's attacks had hammered the Federals away from Richmond, a city so vital in industry, transportation, and political significance that without it the Confederacy had little hope of survival.

The Union general with all of the advantages had been forced into embarrassing retreat. Lee, with the odds stacked heavily against him, had taken hair-raising risks and repelled the invader. A quiet, taciturn, gentleman-soldier had turned the tide of the Civil War. Richmond was safe for the moment, the spirits of the Southern people were high again. In the heat and stench and sickness of the Virginia Peninsula, Lee had wrested victory of sorts from the jaws of almost-certain defeat.

His management had not been flawless, by any means. At Gaines' Mill and Malvern Hill, Lee had hurled his men against formidable defenses. Equally as destructive, Lee demonstrated a propensity to leave the intricacies of battle to his lieutenants. His orders were so few—and Jackson's obedience to commands so thorough—that the latter held his position on three separate days when others expected him to come to their assistance.

Lee had not learned yet how to use Jackson. Once they became more accustomed to the thoughts and expectations of each other, they would work beautifully in concert. Those opportunities would come because of Lee's daring in the Seven Days. He destroyed the Northern hope of a short civil war. With Lee now at the helm, it would be an all-out struggle in which both sides would bring to bear their full capabilities.

Before the end of July, another major Union force moved into Virginia. Gen. John Pope had come swaggering out of the west and taken command of some sixty thousand Federals scattered all across the northern part of the Old Dominion. Pope's charge was to mold these discordant parts into a smoothly functioning whole as he led them on an offensive through the Virginia Piedmont. Whatever strong points Pope had, organization and strategy were not among them.

His stormy tenure began with brash proclamations to his soldiers. Next came a series of declarations. The Federal army would live off the country, Pope announced. Civilians who displayed resistance or disrespect would be subject to severe punishment, including execution. Then this loudmouthed braggart led his army southward up the line of the Orange and Alexandria Railroad, ostensibly to descend on Richmond from the northwest.

The era when Confederates spoke of "chivalrous enemies" was at an end. Pope gained the dubious honor of being the only Union general for whom Lee expressed open contempt. The Confederate general once asserted that Pope needed to be "suppressed"—as if he were some kind of insect to be squashed on sight.

Pope and McClellan genuinely disliked each other, and this was the prelude to their

On June 30, 1862, a Richmond artilleryman was witness to one of the first meetings between Lee and Jackson. Confederates were driving McClellan's army southward. The conference between the two Southern generals was, as always, short and direct. Jackson then saluted and left to take his divisions toward White Oak Swamp.

lack of cooperation and defeat. At the outset, Lee's force stood caught in the middle between the two enemy hosts. Lee could not give primary attention to Pope because McClellan and his one hundred thousand troops were still ominously encamped on the peninsula. Yet the fight had gone out of McClellan.

When the Union commander early in July ordered his troops into encampment rather than to resume the advance on Richmond, one of McClellan's best division leaders snarled in disgust: "We ought instead of retreating to follow up the enemy and take Richmond. . . . I say to you all, such an order can only be prompted by cowardice or treason."

Lee sensed the inertia of the Union army. McClellan "is uneasy in his position," Lee told Davis. The army commander decided to send Jackson with three divisions to delay or defeat Pope in central Virginia. Such a move, Lee thought, would "change the theatre of war" from Richmond to the Virginia Piedmont—which ran all the way to the Potomac River and Washington.

This was a remarkable move on Lee's part from another point of view. He was sending Jackson, not Longstreet, Harvey Hill, Powell Hill, or some other field leader. Jackson had hardly lived up to his reputation in the Seven Days battles. Yet Lee knew a soldier when he saw one. He certainly was going to be generous in dealing with a patriot who had electrified the nation in the Shenandoah Valley. Jackson deserved another chance, and Lee felt comfortable giving it to him. Old Jack departed the Richmond line in mid-July and established a base at the vital railroad junction of Gordonsville.

Jackson's presence in the Piedmont raised anew Union alarm for the safety of Washington. McClellan's persistent claims of Lee in his front with the largest army on the continent now worked against him. The Lincoln administration did not want so huge a force positioned between the two Federal wings. The thing to do was to fuse the two Union armies into one. So over his loud protests, McClellan received orders to withdraw from the peninsula, return to the Washington area as expeditiously as possible, and merge his forces with those of Pope.

The Army of the Potomac was in transit for the better part of a month. That was when Jackson began praying harder and looking for a fight. He learned that the unsupported center of Pope's command had moved to the south of Culpeper. Jackson promptly advised Lee that he was advancing to meet the threat. Lee gave his full endorsement. "I hope you may be able to strike him moving, or at least be able to draw him from his strong positions," the commander wrote. "Relying upon your judgment, courage, and discretion, and trusting to the continued blessing of an ever-kind Providence, I hope for victory."

On August 9, Jackson delivered a furious assault at Cedar Mountain. The Federals made an unexpectedly stiff resistance and even succeeded in crushing Jackson's left flank in the process. However, the Confederates enjoyed a heavy advantage in numbers on the field. By nightfall Jackson had routed that portion of Pope's army. Union losses were 2,400 of 8,000 engaged, while Jackson suffered 1,300 casualties among 20,000 troops at hand.

When Pope began funneling reinforcements toward the Cedar Mountain region the next day, Jackson retired to Gordonsville to await further orders. Pope characteristically misjudged Jackson's withdrawal. Throughout this entire campaign, Pope remained convinced that the Confederates were always trying to get away from him.

Jackson did not remain alone at Gordonsville. McClellan's abandonment of the

As a cold rain poured the day after the end of the Seven Days battles, President Davis met with his weary generals in a private home near the Malvern Hill battlefield. With Longstreet standing in front of the fire and Stuart to Lee's left, the army commander said, "Mr. President, this is our Stonewall Jackson." Davis and the "Victor of the Valley" exchanged respectful looks.

peninsula freed Lee from the Richmond defenses. He hastened west with Gen. James Longstreet's divisions. The boastful Pope grew silent. Suddenly he was facing the full Army of Northern Virginia. That was only the first surprise.

It was imperative to Lee that he finish off Pope before McClellan's army arrived on the scene. Just as Lee had divided his small army in June to initiate the Seven Days, and did the same thing in July to block Pope, now he proposed to split his forces a third time in three months. Again he was taking a strong gamble, for he was temporarily exposing each segment of his smaller army to separate destruction. "The disparity of numbers between the contending forces rendered the risk unavoidable," Lee stated. Put in simple terms, he opted to gamble with action rather than face certain defeat by inaction.

On Sunday afternoon, August 24, near the hamlet of Jeffersonton, a dramatic council of war took place. Lee spread a map on a table placed in the middle of a bare field. Seated on either side of Lee were Generals Longstreet and Stuart. Jackson stood in front of the army chief. No other officers were within hearing distance. Some difference of opinion exists over who conceived the strategy. The authorship is inconsequential. Both Lee and Jackson understood the necessity for swift—and even unorthodox—action if they were to get the better of Pope.

Ignoring the superior numbers of his enemy, Lee was sending Jackson and half of the Confederate army on a wide sweep around Pope's right flank. Jackson's goal was the Orange and Alexandria Railroad, Pope's umbilical cord with both Washington and his supplies. Once the Union general turned to react to Jackson's presence, Lee would move forward and strike Pope from the opposite direction.

A determined Jackson marched away without fanfare. His route was north behind the cover of the Bull Run Mountains, then east through Thoroughfare Gap to Manassas Junction. Jackson's division covered fifty-six miles in two days without encountering Federals. At Bristoe Station

on the Orange and Alexandria line, Confederates scattered a Union guard before wrecking several supply trains passing at a time when the crews had no idea any Confederates were within miles of the railroad.

Jackson quickly pointed his troops seven miles down the tracks to Manassas Junction, the major Union army supply depot. There they found tons of every sort of food hungry Southerners could crave. Confederates gorged themselves with unfamiliar delicacies, carried away everything they could, and applied the torch to the rest. The billowing smoke was visible for thirty miles. In one fell swoop, Jackson had cut Federal supply lines and destroyed the enemy's principal reservoir of ammunition and stores.

A confused and angry Pope had to retreat. He turned to grapple with Jackson under the old assumption that the Confederates were on the run. On August 28, Jackson ambushed the Federal van at Groveton, then backed off a couple of miles to a secure position on high ground and along an unfinished railroad cut. The site overlooked the Manassas battlefield of a year earlier.

Pope arrived and made little or no reconnaissance before sending line after line into attacks on Jackson's position. For two days the fighting, bleeding, and killing continued unabated. "God, Jackson, and our own hearts were our dependence," a South Carolina soldier declared.

So quietly that Pope did not even know it, Lee reunited his divided army on the field of battle. Pope had just telegraphed Washington that he was on the threshold of victory over Jackson when thirty thousand fresh Confederates under Longstreet drove into the exposed Union flank. The Federal army went to pieces again along Bull Run. Lee and Jackson hotly pursued the fleeing enemy. Jackson undertook another curling march in an attempt to inflict a deathblow on Pope's demoralized forces.

The Confederates were too exhausted to maintain a normal marching rate. In a driving rainstorm on September 1, Jackson attacked the Union rear guard and fought to a standstill at Chantilly. Lee was then aware that McClellan's army was arriving from the peninsula. He called off the offensive. Pope's force of some 60,000 troops had taken 16,000 casualties; the Confederate losses in killed, wounded, and missing was 9,200 of 55,000 soldiers. The Southern army was back on the Potomac River, precisely where it had been when the fighting began a year earlier.

All the doubts about Jackson in the Seven Days had now vanished. His role in the Second Manassas campaign had been extraordinary. A London newspaperman traveling with Lee's army wrote of Jackson: "They who have seen and heard him uplift his voice in prayer, and then have witnessed his vigor and prompt energy in the strife, say that once again Cromwell is walking the earth and leading his trusting and enraptured hosts to assured victory."

Only Jackson among Lee's subordinates could have performed as he did. In the six weeks leading up to the actual fighting near Manassas, Jackson's relationship with the main Southern army would have taxed the endurance of any other general. From July 16 to August 15, he was on his own at Gordonsville and Cedar Mountain. During August 15–25, Jackson was part of Lee's maneuvering army. Then, in the critical four days of August 25–29, Jackson again was on his own. He and Lee came back together again for the climax of Second Manassas.

History also contained no parallel to what had taken place in Virginia during the past ninety

LEE'S HAT

days. On June 1, Robert Lee had taken command of a small, disorganized army driven by a massive enemy to the gates of Richmond, and once that city fell, the war would end. Three months later, by the end of August, Lee had whipped the army facing him. Spearheaded by Jackson, he had whipped a second army sent to the relief of the first. Lee had transferred the Civil War from the vicinity of Richmond to the outskirts of Washington. Under Lee's leadership, a Confederate force on the edge of defeat in late spring stood in midsummer at the door to victory. A Confederate artillery officer wrote in awe that Lee was "silent, inscrutable, strong, like a God."

After Second Manassas, Confederates poked among the wreckage in search of food and clothing. The question for Lee was: what next? A variety of choices existed and made the problem more complex. Lee's ultimate solution was sound, although it resulted in the bloodiest single day of the war.

Lee reached his decision by narrowing the choices. He could not attack the fixed defenses of Washington. They were simply too strong. Nor could he wait for the Federals to reorganize and come out against him in force. At the same time, Lee could not keep his hungry and destitute soldiers in a stationary position at Manassas. War had stripped the area of food and forage, and the lines of communication with Richmond were long. Any Confederate march to the east, west, or south would be a retroactive movement that would give up much that had been gained. It would also permit a renewal of Union pressure, first in central Virginia and eventually on Richmond.

Hence, by elimination, Lee determined to take the war to the enemy in his own land. Lee would fight to win by invading the North. Many factors seemed to dictate such an action.

On the north bank of the Potomac was Maryland, a sister state rather than enemy territory. There Lee could possibly obtain supplies from districts untouched by war. He hoped that thousands of Maryland sons would come forth to enlist and join friends and relatives in the

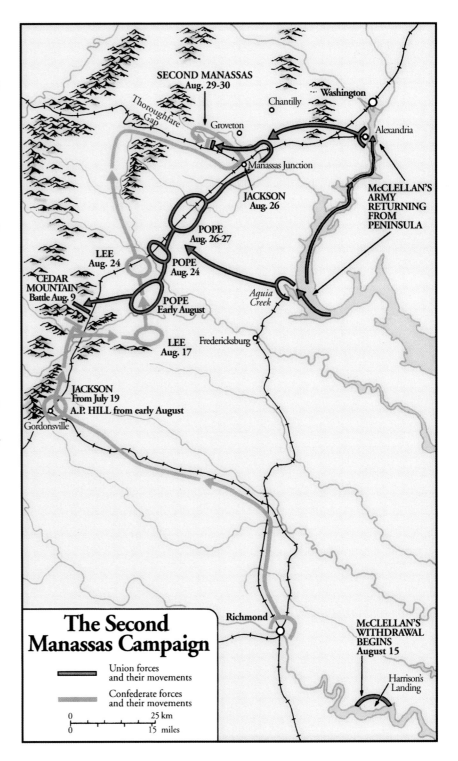

Rain was falling on the morning of August 31, 1862, and the Union army was retiring in defeat from the field at Second Manassas. Lee and Jackson rode across Bull Run and through the woods to get a firsthand view of Federal activities. Musketry from Union pickets soon halted the reconnaissance.

Southern army. (Lee was wrong in every assumption about Maryland.)

The invasion would surely draw off Federals from Virginia and permit the Old Dominion to catch its breath while farmers gathered in the late-summer crops unmolested. Lee's advance would force the Union army to give pursuit. A moving enemy was always likely to make a mistake or get into an awkward situation. Lee would be ready to exploit that error.

In addition, an overriding factor was present, one that stretched far beyond the eastern theater. Lee's two campaigns to date against superior numbers had won for the Confederates the admiration of the world. England seemed on the verge of granting official recognition to the Southern nation; France hovered not too far behind. A third successful campaign, on enemy soil, might bring foreign recognition and aid which, many Confederate leaders had known from the start, was the best assurance that the "second American revolution," like the first, would be triumphant.

On Friday, September 5, with Stuart's cavalry acting as a screen, the Army of Northern Virginia began wading across the Potomac at the shoals near Leesburg. This army was weaker than it would be at any time of the war except for the final weeks. Thousands of Southern soldiers were absent because of wounds, sickness, and exhaustion. Hundreds of others had balked at invasion on the grounds that they had enlisted only to defend their homelands. They now simply walked away from the army rather than be termed invaders.

Only forty thousand men followed Lee into Maryland. They represented barely two-thirds of his army. Most of them were barefooted; all were in rags and hungry. Yet they were the hard core of the South's premier fighting force. One officer noted with open affection, "None but the heroes were left."

Not only was the Confederate army dangerously weak, its high command was hurting. In the first stage of the advance, Lee's horse jerked in fright one morning while the commander was holding the reins. Lee fell to ground and reached out instinctively to cushion the impact. The accident broke one hand and badly sprained the other. Throbbing pain accompanied Lee through most of the ensuing campaign.

Jackson had suffered a similar injury. He mounted a new horse presented to him by grateful Marylanders. When Jackson applied the spur, the animal reared suddenly and fell backward. Jackson plunged to the ground on his back, and the horse fell on top of him. The general was so sore from the fall that he rode into Maryland in an ambulance wagon.

Lee's other corps commander, James Longstreet, had a huge blister on his heel. It kept ripping open through accident and was becoming infected. Longstreet was noticeably impaired. Command structure was literally limping as the critical invasion of the North got under way.

The army halted at Frederick, a Maryland hub from which roads fanned out in every direction. Lee rested his men while he reviewed activity relative to his advance. He was not overly concerned about any enemy pressure. McClellan's army, Lee told a subordinate, "will not be prepared for offensive operations—or he will not think it so—for three or four weeks. Before that time I hope to be on the Susquehanna."

What bothered Lee at the moment was a garrison of eleven thousand Federals at Harpers Ferry. He had expected it to abandon the post when he headed into Maryland, but it did not. Now those Federals posed the threat of disrupting Lee's communications and blocking a probable retirement route into the Shenandoah Valley. Harpers Ferry must be secured before the Confederate army continued farther north.

In enemy country, but seemingly oblivious to dangers, Lee once more divided his army—not in half but in four parts. Immediately to the west was South Mountain, a sharp ridge that began at the Potomac as a continuation of Virginia's Blue Ridge Mountains and ran in a long slant northward for sixty-five miles. Lee with Longstreet's command would cross South

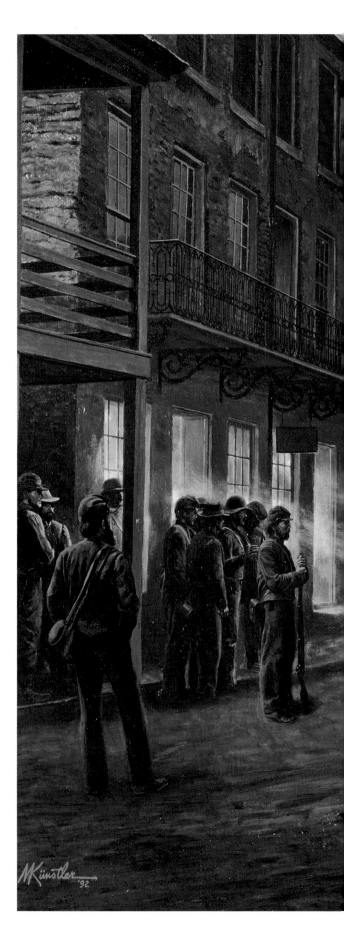

Jackson's accomplishments as an infantry commander make it easy to forget that his basic brilliance—and first love— was artillery. On September 15, 1862, he forced the surrender of the large Federal garrison at Harpers Ferry with a well-placed and concentrated fire from his batteries. His entry into the Ferry a few hours later was unpretentious but victorious.

Mountain and march to Hagerstown to confront a possible threat from Pennsylvania militia. Jackson, with two wings of the army, would go down and attack Harpers Ferry from different directions. Gen. D. H. Hill's division would man the South Mountain openings through which roads from Washington and Frederick snaked to the west.

A day after these movements were under way, the Federal army eased into Frederick. Lee's presence on Northern soil had forced McClellan to give pursuit with unaccustomed vigor. Union soldiers occupied the same campsites that Confederates had used only a few days earlier. That explains how an Indiana soldier accidentally chanced upon a copy of Lee's orders (discarded by a careless Confederate officer). McClellan was suddenly the beneficiary of the greatest security leak in American military history.

Not only did he learn of the Confederates' being split into four parts; he knew where each segment was and where it was expected to be in the days ahead. Moreover, and from his position at Frederick, McClellan was closer to Jackson and closer to Lee than the two Southern commanders were to each other. If McClellan advanced quickly with his full army, the destruction of Lee's comparatively little army piece by piece could be accomplished.

Gnawing self-doubts began to infect the Union commander. Perhaps the "lost order" was a plant; Lee's army might be lying in ambush on the other side of South Mountain; a heavily reinforced Confederate army was hoping that the Union general would take the bait . . .

McClellan spent an entire day carefully getting everything arranged just so. He sent a corps to the aid of the Harpers Ferry garrison while he moved cautiously with the rest of the army toward Boonsboro Gap. Throughout September 14, Confederate defenders—outnumbered five-to-one—waged a Thermopylae-like defense atop South Mountain. They abandoned the heights under darkness and retired to unite with Lee's main body. The Southern commander was now aware that McClellan had a copy of his orders. Lee desperately began gathering the pieces of his army for a major battle.

The next morning, after a skillful deployment of his artillery, Jackson had started an annihilating bombardment of the Harpers Ferry post. Its

The Maryland Campaign

- Union forces and their movements
- Confederate forces and their movements

Hagerstown
Antietam Creek
BATTLE OF ANTIETAM Sept. 17
Sharpsburg
Boonsboro
TURNER'S GAP
BATTLE OF SOUTH MOUNTAIN Sept. 14
SOUTH MOUNTAIN
CRAMPTON'S GAP
LEE Sept. 7
Frederick
McCLELLAN Sept. 13
Harpers Ferry Captured Sept. 15
Shenandoah River
BLUE RIDGE MTS.
LEE crossing Potomac Sept. 4-6
MARYLAND
VIRGINIA
POTOMAC RIVER
Chantilly
LEE Sept. 2-3
Centreville
McCLELLAN
WASHINGTON

0 5 10 15 km
0 5 10 miles

commanding officer quickly struck the white flag. The spoils included 11,000 Federal prisoners, 13,000 small arms, 72 pieces of artillery, 200 wagons, plus tons of commissary and quartermaster stores.

A dusty, uninspiring-looking Jackson rode down the main street of Harpers Ferry after the surrender. One captured Federal studied Jackson for a moment and concluded that he really did not look like much. Then the man added bitterly: "But if we had him we wouldn't be in the fix we're in."

With Jackson's capture of Harpers Ferry, Lee realized that it was not necessary to make a hasty retreat to Virginia. He determined to reassemble the army at Sharpsburg, a dozen miles south of Hagerstown, and make a fight of it. Jackson could reach that village quicker. A victory would enable Lee to continue his drive north. Equally as important were the terrain advantages. Sharpsburg stood on hills overlooking sluggish Antietam Creek. The Potomac River was at Lee's back.

On September 16, half of the Confederate army was trying to unite with the other half. If McClellan had ordered a Union advance all along the line, Lee's forces would unquestionably have been driven into the Potomac. Yet Lee bluffed his enemy with an elaborate but superficial show of force. While McClellan thought about strategy, slowly brought up his guns, discussed dispositions with his generals, and pondered the possibilities of defeat, Lee used the twenty-four hours to get most of his army in position.

Rain during the night of September 16–17 proved an omen to the unprecedented carnage that followed. America in 1862 contained only thirty-five cities that had as many people as were casualties that one day along Antietam Creek.

Predawn fog encased the countryside when the gunfire started. Twelve hours of unremitting violence swept across fields and through woods; sheets of musketry unmercifully cut attacking columns to shreds while artillery indiscriminately destroyed the countryside. Men fell at the rate of almost two thousand per hour.

Antietam began with a concentrated assault on the left of Lee's line. In command of that sector was Stonewall Jackson, who earned anew his nickname that day. His men were in a cornfield and two woodlands in front of a whitewashed Dunker church. A full Federal corps, backed up by three dozen cannon, smashed the cornfield into fodder as Union infantry made for the high ground where the church stood. Confederate units there, many of them experiencing casualties as high as 50 percent of their strength, refused to budge and were mangled beyond recognition. Southern reinforcements finally drove back the Federal attackers, who had lost fully a fourth of their number.

The second hour of combat in Jackson's front brought another charge by a full Federal corps attempting to sever the Confederate line. In this fighting, the cornfield and the woods changed hands twice; officers and privates were strewn everywhere in death or pain. The fighting paused with nothing accomplished except a pathetic thinning of ranks on both sides.

McClellan then sent a third corps against Jackson. Three Federal divisions moved forward, but in the smoke and confusion, troops veered in the wrong direction and were hit in flank and rear by a fresh detachment of Confederates who had come to help Jackson. Somewhere around

THE FLAG OF THE STONEWALL BRIGADE

9 A.M., the fighting in Jackson's front wound down to skirmish fire. It was only midmorning, but a full battle had been waged for insignificant patches of Maryland countryside. The fighting ended precisely where it had begun.

For the remainder of that Wednesday, the slaughter continued at other points along Lee's line. The Confederate center held after hours of fighting for control of nothing more than a sunken lane below the brow of a hill. Union troops finally captured the road, but Lee's line constricted and remained intact.

That afternoon McClellan unleashed heavy assaults against Lee's sapped right flank. Billy Yanks fought their way to the crest of the Confederate position and appeared on the verge at last of fracturing Lee's line. Then the most important reinforcements of the day arrived: A. P. Hill's division, which, after securing Harpers Ferry, had double-timed seventeen miles and ripped into the exposed Federal flank at the last possible moment. This powerful attack broke McClellan's left, saved the Army of Northern Virginia, and ended the battle.

Lee's ten thousand losses at Antietam represented a fourth of his army, but his line miraculously had held. McClellan, with thirteen thousand casualties, still had vastly superior numbers on his side. All logic dictated that Lee withdraw under cover of night. However, Lee pulled his frayed ranks together and calmly waited for McClellan to renew the assaults the next day.

The Union commander spent September 18 wondering why Lee was still there and whether the Union army should attack the next day, the next week, or at all. After sundown, Lee slowly

The first Union onslaught at Antietam came against Jackson's troops, posted around the Dunker church. The general wrote of this bloody action, "With heroic spirit our lines . . . maintained their position in the face of superior numbers, with stubborn resolution. . . . The courage on both sides was terrific." In no battle of the war did Jackson more deserve the sobriquet "Stonewall."

began the southward march to Virginia. His defiant stand after so bloody a battle did much to restore morale in his battered army, and when McClellan allowed the Confederates to recross the Potomac unmolested, Lee's men returned home with feelings that they had won a victory of sorts.

The battle was a tactical draw, but for the Confederates it was a strategic defeat. Lee had gone north with high hopes of ending the war by one grand stroke. His crippled army limped back to Virginia with those hopes shattered. Yet McClellan's failure was equally as great.

Several times he had victory in his grasp, only to lose it by faulty generalship and timidity. At Antietam, never more than twenty thousand Federals went into action at any given time. This enabled Lee to display brilliance in shifting units along inner lines of defense to threatened points. A full twenty thousand Federal soldiers—more than a fourth of McClellan's army—were scarcely engaged at all.

Pitifully, McClellan convinced himself that he had been completely successful. He happily informed his wife after the struggle: "Those in whose judgment I rely tell me that I fought the battle splendidly and that it was a masterpiece of art." Such bluster notwithstanding, Antietam sapped the final potential from McClellan the general.

It had always been a gentleman's war for Little Mac, until he walked over the Antietam battleground and saw firsthand untold numbers of dead and dying soldiers. Any killer instinct he may have had vanished at that moment. McClellan had no intention of doing battle again.

Confusion marked the predawn hours of September 19 as the Confederate army recrossed the Potomac. Mud from recent rains and a single river ford produced a massive traffic jam that gave both Lee and Jackson some apprehension. When Jackson's quartermaster untangled the mess and the last soldiers reached the Virginia shore, Lee exclaimed, "Thank God!"

In October, Lee reorganized his army into two officially constituted corps. It was natural that half of the army would go to Jackson. Between the two generals had now developed a harmonious and trusting relationship. Lee wrote of his lieutenant: "I have only to intimate to him what I wish done, and he promptly obeys my wishes." Jackson's praise of Lee was unusually superlative: "His perception is as quick and unerring as his judgment is infallible . . . General Lee is a phenomenon. . . . So great is my confidence in him that I am willing to follow him blindfolded."

Less than a month later, the Union army also underwent reorganization at the top. Ambrose E. Burnside succeeded the vacillating McClellan as commander of the Army of the Potomac. A stout, easygoing, adopted son of Rhode Island, Burnside was likable and well meaning. He compensated for premature baldness with a fantastic set of whiskers that made a double parabola from in front of his ears, down over his jaws, and up across his mouth. Burnside's most distinguishable trait as a general was limited talent, which he freely acknowledged. He would move from disaster to disaster with uncomprehending dignity.

While Burnside bowed to Northern public pressure and made quick plans for a new offensive, Lee had his army spread defensively all across northern Virginia. Longstreet's corps stood directly in Burnside's front. Jackson's half of the army roamed his familiar haunts at the northern end of the Shenandoah Valley.

Burnside saw no way to do battle with Lee in the present positions. The new army commander decided on a long and secret sweep to his left. A forty-mile march southeast would bring his army to the Rappahannock River and the town of Fredericksburg. By crossing the water barrier quickly and getting between a surprised Lee and Richmond, Burnside would hold the clear advantage. Everything, of course, depended on prompt movements by all components of the Union army.

The plan worked well for a day or so. Burnside had already reached the Fredericksburg area before

On Saturday night, November 29, 1862, Jackson arrived at Fredericksburg from the Valley. Lee greeted his lieutenant at his headquarters with more cordiality than usual. The full Union army was preparing to cross the Rappahannock River. With snow on the ground and cold wind blowing, the two generals studied maps for a new and unusual winter showdown with the enemy.

Lee was aware of the shift. Getting across the river was the next step—and at that point the Union offensive bogged down helplessly. Burnside had to have pontoon bridges to take his troops over the Rappahannock. The pontoons were not waiting for him, as expected. In fact, it would be a month before they reached Fredericksburg.

Fredericksburg

Union forces and their movements

Confederate forces and their movements

Pontoon bridges

0 ½ 1
Mile

Burnside would have been well advised to develop a new plan. Yet he stubbornly resolved to wait and to follow through with his original strategy. Fredericksburg had been all but defenseless when the Union army arrived. By the time Burnside was ready to cross the river in the second week of December, the full Army of Northern Virginia was spread along the forward slope of the ridge behind the town.

Lee had moved quickly to Fredericksburg once he learned of Burnside's advance. His engineering eye saw immediately that the elevated land three-quarters of a mile back from the river was a near-perfect defensive position: it was high enough to provide a clear field of fire and it was low enough to invite attack.

Getting his full army back together again was no easy task for Lee. The weather had turned wintry. Jackson's corps was in the Valley; he wanted to stay there and protect his adopted region. Yet Lee needed him. The Lee-Jackson cooperation never shone more vividly than in a November 20 letter the army commander sent. Lee stated to Jackson: "If you see no way of making an impression on the enemy from where you are, and concur with me in the view I have expressed, I wish you would move east of the Blue Ridge, and take such actions as you may find best."

This was a remarkable communiqué. Lee felt strongly that his two corps should be together at Fredericksburg, but his confidence in Jackson's judgment was such that he left the decision to his subordinate. Further, with battle all but imminent, Lee gave Jackson the option of undertaking any offensive he desired once he was east of the mountains.

Burnside had to fight his way into Fredericksburg. His troops took part of the tardy pontoons, filled them with infantry, and paddled across the river under a hail of Confederate musketry. Federals fought from street to street, house to house, as they cleared the town. It took the Army of the Potomac the better part of a day to file across bridges and into Fredericksburg. Open ground

Federal troops were massing to attack at Fredericksburg. Lee and Jackson, accompanied by Maj. Heros von Borcke, one of Stuart's aides, crept to within four hundred yards of the Union army to get a better view of enemy dispositions. Von Borcke confessed extreme nervousness that the three officers were "so close to the enemy, who surely little suspected that the two greatest heroes of the war were so nearly in their clutches."

stood between the residential streets and what was called Marye's Heights. Once Burnside got his army across the Rappahannock, nothing remained for it to do but to attack.

Lee posted Longstreet's troops on the left, atop the highest ground. The center of Longstreet's sector overlooked the town. Jackson's men on the right took battle position on a slight rise that ended at Hamilton's Crossing on the Richmond, Fredericksburg, and Potomac Railroad. Lee's line was a full seven miles long, but it was as strong a front as he mustered during the war. Men and guns were banked in rows. On Longstreet's front, a sunken road ran alongside a stone wall and formed a natural breastwork. Wherever Federals attacked, they would have to charge up an incline. Although the word is often overused, one can say unequivocally that at Fredericksburg, Lee's position was impregnable.

Union soldiers saw that fact, although Burnside did not. He arranged half of his army in front of Jackson, the other half facing Longstreet, and ordered them forward in a two-pronged attack. More than one hundred thousand Federals surged forward, the Confederates opened fire, and a veritable massacre began. The outcome was rarely in doubt.

Downriver, an unsupported Union assault actually punctured Jackson's position momentarily. However, a vicious counterattack sent Federals racing back across the field, taking heavy casualties as they withdrew. In Longstreet's sector, despite more than a dozen separate assaults, no Union soldier got within one hundred yards of the sunken road. A seemingly oblivious Burnside kept ordering charge after charge. Near sundown a Union corps commander stated bitterly: "Finding that I had lost as many men as my orders required me to lose, I suspended the attack."

Meanwhile, atop Marye's Heights, Lee watched the Union army melt away from concentrated gunfire and observed sadly: "It is well that war is so terrible; else we should grow too fond of it."

More than thirteen thousand Federals were killed or wounded at Fredericksburg. Losses in

AT LEFT:
Early on the morning of the battle of Fredericksburg, Jackson appeared not in familiar, weather-beaten clothes but in a new uniform with conspicuous general's braid. Soldiers cheered heartily as "Old Jack" moved to battle in the full regalia of a corps commander. Riding in front with Jackson in this painting are Stuart and Lee. Behind them are Longstreet and a color guard.

OVERLEAF:
On January 20, 1863, Lee rode to Moss Neck (Jackson's headquarters) to review the cavalry brigade of his son, Gen. W. H. F. "Rooney" Lee. Several generals, including Jackson and Stuart, accompanied the army chief down a line of horsemen thin in number but still determined in spirit.

Lee's army were a third of that number. The next day, hundreds of dead Yankees lay naked and gleaming in the cold December sunlight. Ragged Confederates had gone onto the field under cover of darkness to secure warm uniforms and shoes that their opponents no longer needed.

The two armies then went into winter quarters, with only the Rappahannock dividing friend from foe. Sickness and suffering became common denominators on both sides, but more so for the ill-equipped Confederates. Food was scarce and often primitive, replacement uniforms nonexistent, horses emaciated, accouterments in disrepair. Unit commanders replenished as best they could.

Lee had an occasional parade or review in an effort to sustain morale. On Sundays, and sometimes on weekdays, religious services were held inside the Army of Northern Virginia. Lee and Jackson often prayed side by side at church meetings as they sought divine help to overcome earthly tribulations.

In February 1863, on the other side of the Rappahannock River, a Union general at last received his wish to lead the Army of the Potomac. Joseph Hooker was forty-eight and the most handsome commander the army would ever have. Square-shouldered, erect, with blue eyes and an abundance of blond hair, Fighting Joe had been an 1837 graduate of West Point and one of the most decorated soldiers in the Mexican War. His Civil War record to that point was solid.

There was also a dark side to Hooker. Ambition burned brightly. So did hard drinking and womanizing. Charles Francis Adams wrote that Hooker's tent was a place to which no gentleman cared to go and to which no lady would go. Still, the New England general got off to a good start as army commander.

Hooker's first acts were to remove all the causes of low morale. He improved rations, granted more liberal furloughs, found six months' back pay for his soldiers, and created badges for divisions to build unit pride. By spring, Hooker had 134,000 trained, well-conditioned, fully equipped soldiers, including 10,000 cavalry

mounted on fine horses and 400 of the best cannon that American technology could produce. Hooker loudly pronounced his command to be "the finest army on the planet."

Fellow Union generals nevertheless knew that Hooker was self-confident to the point of being self-righteous. Such an attitude worried President Lincoln, who remarked to Hooker that "the hen is the wisest of all the animal creation because she never cackles until the egg is laid."

As winter snows melted, Lee of necessity dispatched Longstreet and most of his corps to southeast Virginia for patrol duty and food gathering. That left Lee's tattered army woefully outnumbered. The spring campaign would open with the Federal army having all of the advantages. The real contest, however, was going to be between two commanders who did not know one another and who would never come within miles of seeing each other in the struggle about to commence.

Hooker believed with all his heart that the spring 1863 battle plan he had developed against Lee could not fail. The Union general had no intention of crossing the Rappahannock River and butting heads with Lee. Hapless Ambrose Burnside had already shown the disaster inherent in such strategy.

What Hooker had in mind was to take seventy thousand soldiers, march some twenty-five miles upriver, cross both the Rappahannock and Rapidan Rivers, and then swing down on Lee's left flank and rear. The remaining portion of the

Lee and Jackson often attended religious services together. They both felt what Lee expressed to his wife: "My heart is filled with gratitude to Almighty God for his unspeakable mercies. . . . What should have become of us without His crowning help and protection?"

JACKSON'S FIELD DESK

Union army, forty thousand men under Gen. John Sedgwick, would occupy Lee's attention at Fredericksburg. Then, if Lee turned to stop Hooker, Sickles would advance on the Confederate army from the opposite direction.

On paper, Lee would be caught in the middle of a contest he could not win. Only two options seemed open to him. Lee could abandon Fredericksburg and retreat southward—in which event Hooker's army would easily strike him in the flank and force Lee to face his enemy on ground of Hooker's choosing. On the other hand, Lee could stand and fight it out at Fredericksburg—a decision that would leave the Southern army pinned between two Federal forces and ultimately squeezed to death by the giant pincer. "My plans are perfect," Hooker chortled. "May God have mercy on General Lee for I will have none."

Attention North and South soon focused on a strange parcel of land in central Virginia. Some ten miles west of Fredericksburg, along the south bank of the Rappahannock, open fields and small woodlands abruptly stopped. In their place was an expanse twelve miles long and six miles wide. It was a silent, forbidding tract of stunted pines, crowded saplings, and heavy underbrush that sprawled across the land and dipped occasionally into irregular ravines. Tiny streams appeared from nowhere and disappeared into somewhere.

Only a handful of cleared settlements broke the thick woods.

The place was dark and sinister even at high noon. Rarely could a person see more than twenty yards ahead. A Union soldier likened the region to a land of grinning ghosts. Locals called it the Wilderness.

There two mighty armies gravitated to continue a war over the future definition of America. Like so many great battles in history, this one would center on a most inconsequential spot on the map: a brick mansion at an intersection of two wagon roads deep in the Wilderness. This simple, isolated crossroads had the imposing name of Chancellorsville.

Hooker unfolded his grand strategy as scheduled. The first stages proceeded smoothly and supposedly in secret. By April 30, four Union corps were jammed together at Chancellorsville. Some fifty thousand troops were ready for action while another twenty thousand were less than a day behind. Yet Hooker had committed a major blunder at the outset by sending his cavalry around Lee's eastern flank to sever Confederate communication and supply lines. The move was designed to cut Lee adrift from his bases to the south of Fredericksburg.

The Union horsemen accomplished little, except to leave Hooker's army blind to whatever reactions Lee might make. Meanwhile, Lee kept his own cavalry under Gen. Jeb Stuart close at hand. Confederate riders alerted Lee to Hooker's whereabouts before the Union commander had completed the second day of his circuitous advance.

From the Confederate point of view, the battle that took place at Chancellorsville was as close to a flawless contest as any engagement ever planned and carried out by an American field general. Robert E. Lee faced an enemy army two and a half times larger than his own, better equipped in every way, and possessed of vastly superior firepower. A skillful advance by Hooker threatened Lee on two fronts. That was the setting when Lee became predictable for doing the unpredictable.

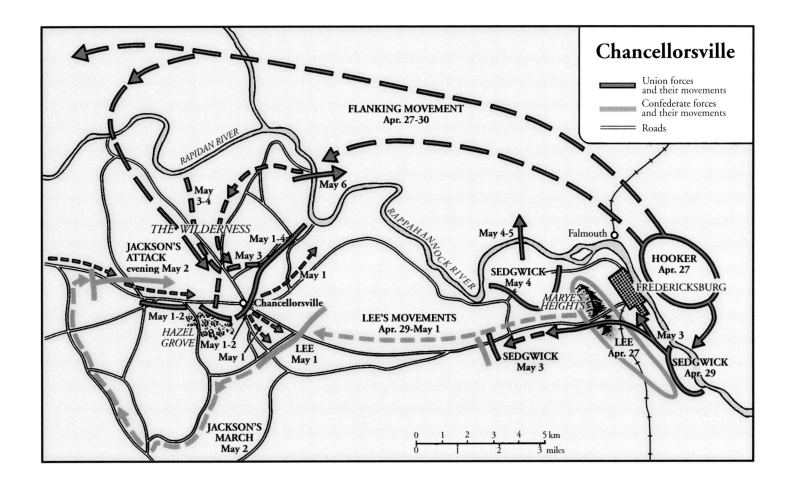

The following labels appear on the map:

Chancellorsville

Union forces and their movements
Confederate forces and their movements
Roads

FLANKING MOVEMENT Apr. 27-30

RAPIDAN RIVER

May 3-4

THE WILDERNESS

JACKSON'S ATTACK evening May 2

May 1-4

May 3

May 1

May 6

RAPPAHANNOCK RIVER

May 4-5   Falmouth

SEDGWICK May 4

HOOKER Apr. 27

FREDERICKSBURG

May 1-2

HAZEL GROVE   May 1-2

May 1

LEE May 1

LEE'S MOVEMENTS Apr. 29-May 1

MARYE'S HEIGHTS

LEE Apr. 27

May 3

Chancellorsville

SEDGWICK May 3

SEDGWICK Apr. 29

JACKSON'S MARCH May 2

0 1 2 3 4 5 km
0   1   2   3 miles

Precisely because he was hopelessly outnumbered, Lee could take preposterous risks. The odds against him were so long at the outset that no damage would be done by lengthening them further. Hence, Lee boldly divided his army in the face of his opponent's strength. Lee left a paltry ten thousand soldiers under hard-fighting Gen. Jubal A. Early to resist Sedgwick's moves at Fredericksburg. The rest of the Army of Northern Virginia started toward Chancellorsville and the larger danger.

Actually, Lee's forces arrived too late to trap Hooker in the dense woods of the Wilderness. Some fifteen to eighteen miles separated Hooker from Sedgwick. To lessen any danger in the gap between them, early on May 1 Hooker ordered his huge Chancellorsville force to march east and shorten the distance. The van of the Union army advanced two miles into open country. Then Hooker made a second—this time fatal—error in judgment.

His lead units had met little more than a single Confederate division blocking the way. Federals prepared to shoulder the roadblock aside, and officers at the front so informed Hooker. Yet the Southerners resisted more fiercely than anticipated. The harder they fought, the more uncertain Hooker became about the enemy's strength. Lacking cavalry reports, he soon concluded that Lee's whole army was at hand. That was when Fighting Joe wilted.

Hooker ordered his troops back to defensive works at the Chancellorsville intersection. This move not only gave up the initiative; worse, it locked most of the Union army in a wooded jungle where maneuvering was restricted, heavy firepower was meaningless, superior numbers were neutralized, and visibility was extremely limited. Hooker the gambler had folded at the critical moment in the game of war.

Jeb Stuart then discovered that the Union right flank, three miles to the west of the

Chancellorsville crossroads, was vulnerable. The line simply ran to the west and came to an end "dangling in the air." It was neither anchored on a strong terrain feature nor was it refused (curved back) to form a defensive perimeter. Hooker's withdrawal into the Wilderness also convinced Lee that the next step was his for the taking. Now it was the turn of Lee the gambler to play his hand.

On the night of May 1–2, Lee and Jackson sat in the woods on cracker boxes. They were barely a half mile from the main Federal lines. From their low-voiced conversation evolved a counterstrategy exciting for its audacity. Lee would flank the army that had been seeking to flank him.

What Lee devised with his principal lieutenant was having Jackson take part of the Confederate army, march the length of Hooker's front, circle around until he was due west of the enemy army, and then assail the exposed right flank. Such a march would consume the better part of a day. Forming a battle line in the trackless expanse of the Wilderness might require more hours. Not much daylight would remain for the assault.

Jackson eagerly accepted the challenge. Lee asked Jackson how many men he wanted to take. "My entire corps," came the quick reply. That would leave Lee with eighteen thousand soldiers to stand for a day or more between Hooker's massive force and the Confederate capital! Lee may have blinked at Jackson's response, but he replied quietly: "Very well. Go ahead."

Lee and Jackson thought alike. If one was going to attempt a flanking movement, then do so in force in order to strike a crippling blow. The decision by Lee to send so large a part of his army on a sweeping march through the unknowns of the Wilderness was perhaps the greatest risk he ever took. If it failed, Richmond, the Confederacy, and the war itself would be lost.

Nighttime still draped the Wilderness as Lee, Jackson, and Stuart made a check of maps in final preparation for what became the most dramatic

The atmosphere was tense on the night of May 1, 1863, as Lee and Jackson conferred deep in the Wilderness west of Fredericksburg. Jeb Stuart soon joined them with the startling news that the right flank of a seventy-thousand-man Union army was unprotected. Lee at once began to consider sending Jackson on another grand sweep around the enemy's line.

flank march of the Civil War. The sun was clearing the eastern horizon when Jackson's corps—28,000 men and 110 guns—set out on a thirteen-mile semicircular movement toward Hooker's flank. Troops marched four abreast on narrow paths and single-lane roads.

Jackson had attended to some last-minute details before mounting Little Sorrel and starting for his accustomed place at the head of his men. He had not ridden a quarter-mile before he spied Lee standing by the side of the road. Jackson reined his horse, saluted, and engaged in a brief exchange with the army commander. Old Jack pointed to the west. Lee nodded. His great lieutenant then rode slowly away. It was the last meeting between the two generals.

Much skirmishing and some fighting occurred during that Saturday. Lee gave a masterly imitation of a commander about to attack from south and east. Hooker braced for the worst from those directions. Meanwhile, Jackson's soldiers marched silently mile after mile on mostly abandoned wagon trails. Late afternoon found Old Jack and most of his men spread through the woods in a battle line a full mile wide.

Billy Yanks on Hooker's far right had no inkling of any pending disturbance. By 5:15, Union soldiers had stacked their arms. Some were napping while others were cooking supper. Two Union bands were playing at the moment. An irony existed in their tunes: "The Girl I Left Behind Me" and "Come Out of the Wilderness."

Suddenly the wild scream of the Rebel Yell and a loud roar of musketry from the west broke the stillness. Thousands of Confederates in three waves descended upon the unprotected Union line. Jackson's men stormed eastward through underbrush so thick that parts of uniforms were ripped away in the assault. At the same time, the Federal corps opposing them had disintegrated into a confused, yelling, running horde of soldiers and horses fleeing in panic.

Here and there, Union regiments or parts of regiments sought to make a stand, but it was hopeless. Confederates swept over them, the

AT RIGHT:

Lee was making the biggest gamble of his military career, and Jackson was embarking on perhaps the most daring flanking movement he had ever undertaken. Yet around 7:30 A.M. on May 2, 1863, both generals were confident of success as they conferred briefly. Neither had a thought that this would be their last meeting.

OVERLEAF:

Darkness and confusion prevailed when Jackson, A. P. Hill, and their staffs rode forward through the woods of Chancellorsville to ascertain the new line of the enemy. As the party galloped back through the dark forest, men in the Eighteenth North Carolina naturally mistook them for Union cavalry and opened fire. Three bullets struck Jackson.

Southern battle line so wide that any point of resistance could be surrounded and overcome with comparative ease. For three miles Jackson cut and slashed as pieces of the Federal right flank fell back into the center of Hooker's line.

Nightfall interrupted the fight and brought widespread confusion. Some thirty thousand men were still locked in some kind of combat; no one really knew where anyone else was. As one Federal soldier confessed, "Darkness was upon us, and Jackson was on us, and fear was on us." Disorder was almost as acute on the other side.

Jackson was not content with the success gained, nor was he concerned about darkness and the dense woods. He was fighting for the Lord, and God's will was fully at work! The destruction of the enemy was at hand. "Press on! Press on!" he shouted.

Sometime near 9:30 P.M., with his staff and some couriers, Jackson rode forward through the timber to reconnoiter. He pinpointed the location of the hastily improvised Union position, then turned and rode back through the dark woods toward his own lines. The always secretive Jackson had told no one where he was going or where he expected to be. As the mounted party came rapidly through the woods from the direction of the enemy lines, troops in one of Jackson's own brigades understandably mistook the riders for Federal cavalry. A Confederate officer yelled, and his men sent a volley of musketry into the faces of the horsemen some twenty yards away.

The mounted party went into a turmoil of death, wounds, frightened horses, shock, and pain. Both of Jackson's arms fell to his side.

By the morning of May 3, 1863, the two wings of Lee's army had reunited and were driving Union forces from Chancellorsville. Lee appeared at the front. Weary Southerners—some blackened by smoke, others limping from wounds—yelled hysterically at the sight of their leader. A staff officer commented, "I thought that it must have been from such a scene that men in the ancient days ascended to the dignity of the gods."

Bullets pierced his forearm and struck a bone in his upper left arm. Another projectile had penetrated his right hand. Eventually litter-bearers bore the badly wounded general to the rear.

Most of the battle of Chancellorsville remained to be fought. The Federals might still have won it. Yet Hooker could not comprehend that forty-two thousand Southerners had "surrounded" his seemingly unbeatable army. So at dawn, May 3, Hooker sat immobile and let the Confederates attack again. That they did: Jackson's troops (under Jeb Stuart) from one direction, Lee's men from another.

Southerners took possession of Hazel Grove, a commanding knoll within artillery distance of the Chancellorsville intersection. Confederate batteries began an effective fire into the center of Hooker's line. The Federal commander was standing on the porch of the Chancellor tavern when a shell struck the pillar against which he was leaning. Dazed more than wounded, Hooker lost all reasoning ability.

He thereupon abandoned much of the field. The Union army huddled in a new line while its general thought only of how to avoid annihilation. This constricting of the Federal lines enabled Lee and Stuart to rejoin forces. Then occurred one of those sublime moments in history that live forever. Col. Charles Marshall, a Confederate staff officer, described it well.

Chancellor House and the woods surrounding it were wrapped in flames. In the midst of this awful scene, General Lee, mounted on [his gray stallion Traveller], rode to the front of his advancing battalions. His presence was the signal for one of those outbursts of enthusiasm which none can appreciate who have not witnessed them.

The fierce soldiers with their faces blackened with the smoke of battle, the wounded crawling with feeble limbs from the fury of the devouring flames, all seemed possessed with a common impulse. One long, unbroken cheer, in which the feeble cry of those who lay helpless on the earth blended with the strong voices of those who still fought, rose high above the roar of battle, and hailed the presence of the victorious chief. He sat in the full realization that soldiers dream of—triumph; and as I looked upon him in the complete fruition of the success which his genius, courage, and confidence in his army had won, I thought that it must have been from such a scene that men in ancient days rose to the dignity of gods.

Chancellorsville was now Lee's battle, and he quickly showed it. Federal General Sedgwick, aware of the onslaught against Hooker, stormed and carried the thin Confederate line at Fredericksburg. Lee had just sent Hooker reeling when he learned that Sedgwick was advancing westward toward his rear. Once again Lee coolly divided his army. He left a small portion to continue stinging Hooker while two divisions marched east to confront Sedgwick.

At Salem Church, six miles from Chancellorsville, Lee attacked from two directions. Sedgwick managed to repulse the assaults, but it cost him forty-seven hundred casualties. In the end, he and his Federals were happy to scamper across the Rappahannock during the night.

Lee turned and went back to finish Hooker. The Union army was still larger and better armed than Lee's forces; it occupied solid earthworks on elevated ground; half of the Federal units had not yet been in action. Nevertheless, Hooker called it quits. On the night of May 6, with rain falling, the "finest army on the planet" dejectedly headed north in defeat.

Hooker had lost 17,287 men killed, wounded, and missing. The plan that could not fail had failed. A stunned Lincoln reacted to the news by exclaiming in anguish: "My God! My God! What will the country say?" The word *Chancellorsville* became a scar on the national memory.

The battle was more than a personal triumph for Lee; it was the most spectacular victory of his career. It elevated him with the great warriors of history. Yet Chancellorsville was in more than one sense a disaster for the South. The almost thirteen thousand Southern losses represented a fourth of Lee's strength. Of equal impact, perhaps, the struggle shattered an unprecedented military partnership.

On hearing that Jackson had fallen wounded, Lee sent him a quick message: "Could I have directed events, I should have chosen for the good of the country to be disabled in your stead."

In the early morning hours of May 3, surgeons amputated Jackson's mangled arm just below the shoulder. The general withstood the loss of a limb with his abiding faith that God's will was at work.

Lee remained extremely concerned, even though he could not bring himself to visit his most dependable soldier. "Give him my affectionate regards," he told Jackson's chaplain, "and tell him to make haste and get well, and come back to me as soon as he can. He has lost his left arm, but I have lost my right arm."

Lee ordered Jackson moved to the nearest railhead for possible transfer to one of the Richmond military hospitals. From the Chancellorsville battlefield to Guiney Station was a twenty-seven-mile wagon ride over rough country roads. Jackson's spirits were high throughout the long and uncomfortable journey. Yet in the days thereafter his condition took a sharp turn for the worse. Physicians had no difficulty making a diagnosis: dreaded pneumonia.

Jackson had always expressed the wish that he might die on the Sabbath. In midafternoon on Sunday, May 10, he emerged from unconsciousness long enough to say: "Let us cross over the river and rest under the shade of the trees." Some final breaths, and a life of thirty-nine years ceased.

In terms of military leadership, the loss of Stonewall Jackson was incalculable. His death was the greatest personal calamity the Confederate nation suffered in the Civil War. The largest crowd ever assembled in Richmond suspended daily life to do him honor. After his body lay in state in the Virginia capitol, a funeral procession wound slowly through the streets of the grief-stricken city. Then family and fellow officers escorted the remains home to Lexington. Jackson's earthly pilgrimage, for God and his beloved state, was done.

PART

IV

Victory

to

Defeat

*Late June 1863 and Lee was carrying the war—and the hopes of
the Southern people—into the North a second time. The army
was passing through Hagerstown, Maryland. A woman standing
by the roadside and defiantly waving an American flag saw Lee
on Traveller and was overcome by the sight of the handsome commander. "Oh," she exclaimed, "I wish he was ours!"*

VICTORY TO DEFEAT

I KNOW NOT HOW TO REPLACE him," a grief-stricken Lee said at Stonewall Jackson's death. Lee's statement was a reflection of the South's loss. Grown men wept in public; mourning descended over every corner of the Confederacy. Yet consuming sorrow had to be pushed aside in the Army of Northern Virginia. Too much needed to be done, and quickly.

The immediate order of business for Lee was filling some of the thirteen thousand gaps left by the victory at Chancellorsville. Officers had to be appointed to higher levels. Shortages in manpower necessitated units consolidating or shrinking in order to close ranks. Of greatest importance to Lee was finding a replacement for Jackson.

No one possessed Jackson's intuitive and collaborative qualities. Lee therefore reached the only possible solution by reorganizing his army from two to three corps. The powerfully built James Longstreet, with his cold gray-blue eyes and heavy beard, continued at the head of the First Corps. Longstreet had a curious self-intoxication about his strategic thinking. Nevertheless, Lee thought him dependable and once referred to Longstreet as "my old war horse." Lee recommended that Gens. Richard S. Ewell and A. Powell Hill be promoted to lieutenant general and given command of a reconstituted Second Corps and newly created Third Corps, respectively.

"Old Bald Head" Ewell was a character even in a war with scores of characters. A professional soldier with twenty-five years' army experience, Ewell was a short man who possessed the toughness of a mule. Glistening dome, bulging eyes, sweeping mustache, and the countenance of a startled bird were combined with awesome profanity fired in a high-pitched voice. By the spring of 1863, two features of Ewell were evident. One was a peg leg, the result of a battle wound the

previous August. The other was the knowledge that Ewell was a solid soldier as long as someone told him exactly what to do.

Powell Hill was more controversial. He was a product of Virginia's landed gentry, a West Point graduate, and—by Lee's statement—the finest division commander in the army. Impetuous and pugnacious in battle, he was intense and sensitive in his relations with fellow officers. The previous year, both Longstreet and Jackson had placed him under arrest for disrespect. Hill had retaliated by seeking to have Jackson court-martialed.

Hill was taller than average but had the nickname "Little Powell" because of a lean frame. He wore his chestnut hair unusually long. The most noticeable facial feature were hazel eyes that flashed in anger or battle. Disdaining formal uniforms, Hill wore civilian garb. He tended to be a loner who never developed intimate friends.

While officers were learning new responsibilities of command, Lee prepared for a second major invasion. He was aware that in spite of

LEE'S HEADQUARTERS FLAG

A product of Virginia Piedmont aristocracy, A. P. Hill (1825–65) became one of the most aggressive generals in Lee's army. Called "Little Powell" because of his thin frame, Hill was impetuous, proud, and sensitive—but so thoroughly devoted to the South that he gave his life for the Confederate cause.

to press quickly over the river, cross western Maryland, and drive into the rich farmland of Pennsylvania. The prime target was Harrisburg, the state capital whose commerce, railroad lines, and river traffic virtually linked the eastern and western theaters.

The Army of Northern Virginia, with Longstreet's corps back in the ranks, numbered about seventy-six thousand men. Lee still believed that his army, if properly led, was unbeatable. His troops fully shared that air of invincibility. A Texas soldier who joined the army that spring commented: "One day's observation has led me to believe that no army on earth can whip these men. They may be cut to pieces and killed, but routed and whipped, never!"

Down in the ranks was a group unity that made Lee's army a swiftly moving and deadly adversary. On the command level, however, was a newness that was dangerous. Two of three corps commanders were learning their jobs; four of twelve division leaders had never commanded soldiers at that level; twelve of the thirty-seven brigadier generals were at the head of brigades for the first time.

Too often overlooked as well in this campaign was the health of Robert E. Lee. The Civil War broke him physically. A month or so earlier, he had suffered the first in a series of heart attacks. Twelve months in the field, directing one campaign after another, had taxed the stamina of the fifty-six-year-old general. In the critical battle that lay ahead, chronic diarrhea would cripple Lee further. He was a sick man without knowing the full extent of his condition.

The invasion unfolded with no major snags except hard marching and hot weather that combined to knock men from the ranks in a steady stream. By the end of June, Ewell's corps was at Carlisle, Pennsylvania. Harrisburg and its many east-west arteries were twenty miles away. Confusion, if not chaos, had spread across the North. Everything was going smoothly for the invaders. Then the first breakdown occurred. It was with Lee's cavalry.

Chancellorsville, the Confederacy was growing weaker by the month. The South could not match the North blow for blow. On the other hand, Lee's victory over Hooker had created demoralization in many parts of the North. A heavy blow, delivered now and aimed at breaking the Federal will to continue the struggle, might obtain the independence that the Confederacy desired.

Additionally, a drive into enemy territory could relieve Federal pressure bearing down hard in the western theater. It would allow Lee to feed his army on the rich countryside in Pennsylvania while Virginia farmers collected their crops without interference. More fundamentally, Lee had to do something. Standing on the defensive in Virginia was akin to waiting for the executioner.

In the first week of June, therefore, advance elements of the Confederate army headed in a wide arc toward the Potomac River one hundred miles upstream from Washington. Lee wanted

On June 9, a large force of Union troopers had surprised Jeb Stuart at Brandy Station. An all-day battle ended in a draw, but for the first time in the war, Federal horsemen had held their own against Southern cavalry. Stuart seethed over his tarnished reputation.

After arriving in Pennsylvania, Stuart took advantage of Lee's loosely worded orders and embarked with a division of cavalry on another ride around the Federal army. The exploit flashed with excitement and resulted in the capture of a Union train of 125 fully loaded wagons. Yet cavalry were the eyes of an army. Without Stuart, Lee stumbled blindly in enemy territory. At one point the commander stated in frustration: "I do not know what to do; I cannot hear from General Stuart."

By then the Army of the Potomac was giving chase. It was doing so under a new commanding general: crusty George G. Meade. He was never an inspiring soldier, but he was high minded and dependable—traits that could not be applied to his predecessors. Meade had sunken eyes, a habitual frown, and an uncontrollable temper. Billy Yanks called him "a damned, goggle-eyed old snapping turtle." Yet Meade was an admirable man void of undermining ambition. That was well, for he had been in command of the army only three days when the most famous battle in American history exploded in rural Pennsylvania.

When Lee heard of the approach of the enemy, he ordered his own forces to concentrate on the east side of the mountains at Cashtown. By June 30, Longstreet and Hill had their corps at the rendezvous. Ewell was marching south from Carlisle. Lee and Meade, old friends from Mexican War days, knew one another well. "General Meade will commit no blunder on my front," Lee stated, "and if I make one he will make haste to take advantage of it."

Reports materialized of a warehouse laden with new shoes eight miles to the east at Gettysburg, a pleasant little town where a number of roads met. The rumors were too enticing for an army half-barefooted to ignore. Powell Hill

ordered a division to march to Gettysburg, brush aside some Union cavalry known to be there, and confiscate the shoes. What the Confederate commanders did not realize was that the Union horsemen consisted of two full brigades under stolid Gen. John Buford. They were the advance of the Army of the Potomac.

Battle exploded on July 1 on a ridge west of Gettysburg. Buford's cavalry stopped the Confederate advance long enough for some of Meade's infantry to move into position. Both armies rushed reinforcements into the area. Combat roared through the morning and into the afternoon. Lines swayed back and forth to the east and west. Then Ewell and his corps, advancing to the sound of the guns, came in from the north and slammed into the Union flank.

Lee's army was consolidating rapidly. Under pressure from two directions and with only part of Meade's army on the field, the Federals began

Despite the fact that two of his kinsmen became Confederate generals, John Buford (1826–63) was one of the North's most dependable cavalry officers. He blunted the enemy's advance on the first day at Gettysburg and bought enough time for the Union army to reach the field. Tragically, Buford died of typhoid fever a few months later.

to give way. The battle swirled through the streets of Gettysburg and out toward high ground south and east of town.

It was strange terrain: a fairly solid ridge in the shape of an inverted question mark. The area in the curved part was called Cemetery Hill because the local burial ground was there. Where the curve ended was steep and wooded Culp's Hill. A long ridge ran south from the cemetery and appropriately had the name of Cemetery Ridge. It ended at two rocky knolls a mile or more away. Little Round Top was the anchor of the ridge. The "period in the question mark" was Big Round Top, too precipitous to be a factor in the battle.

Lee himself reached Gettysburg near midafternoon. He saw instantly that Cemetery Hill commanded the area around it and was lightly defended. The commander directed Ewell to attack the position "if practicable" (a phrase Lee had often used with Jackson), but to avoid

triggering full battle until all of the Confederate army was at hand. Ewell was already having problems being a corps commander. Lee's discretionary orders offered too much latitude. Ewell conferred, considered, weighed each risk involved; while he vacillated, Union troops flooded the hilltop.

Men in the Second Corps who survived the war and made any statements about Gettysburg were unanimous in one belief: had Old Jack been there on July 1, he would have stormed Cemetery Hill in the afternoon, cleared the Federals from the high ground, and won the battle—and perhaps the war as well.

As the fighting ground down for the day, Lee announced that he planned to renew the battle the next morning. Longstreet objected strongly, which was nothing new. The opinionated corps commander had opposed the invasion from the start. Now he believed that the safest move was to

break off the engagement and go back to Virginia. If the Confederates had to fight the next day, he argued, they should try to turn the Federal left rather than make a head-on strike.

Lee remained deaf to all such alternatives. He was deep inside enemy territory. The fight was under way and must be carried to a successful conclusion. Otherwise, the entire campaign was a failure. Longstreet's proposal of a turning movement was out of the question. With Stuart absent, Lee had no idea where the Union flank ended and what might be around and behind it. No, Lee told Longstreet, "If Meade is here tomorrow, I will attack him."

The original plan was for Ewell to make the main effort against the Union right near Culp's Hill. Ewell continued to appear confused and irresolute. Lee decided to use Longstreet for a major assault on the opposite end of the line. Choosing the pessimistic Longstreet to direct an attack seemed a questionable move. Yet Lee had no choice.

Hill's corps had taken a beating the previous day, and Ewell was unreliable. "Old Pete" Longstreet was the senior corps commander, a general who could deliver powerful attacks. Lee was confident that all would be well.

During the moonlit night of July 1–2, most of Meade's eighty-seven thousand soldiers arrived on the scene with the rest coming up fast. Defender outnumbered attacker and held one of the strongest geographical positions in the area. If Lee knew this, he was not overly concerned. His army was invincible. It had shown before that it could be victorious against heavy odds.

Everything that could go wrong went wrong for the Confederates on the second day of combat. Longstreet was to strike the Union left while Hill and Ewell performed diversionary actions along the rest of the line. However, Longstreet's

Lee was such an unpretentious commander that he wore the simplest of uniforms (sometimes disdaining a general's insignia on his collar) and carried with him only a small entourage of aides. To one observer, "Marse Robert" moved along the ranks "as unostentatiously as if he had been the head of a plantation, riding over his fields to . . . give directions about ploughing and seeding."

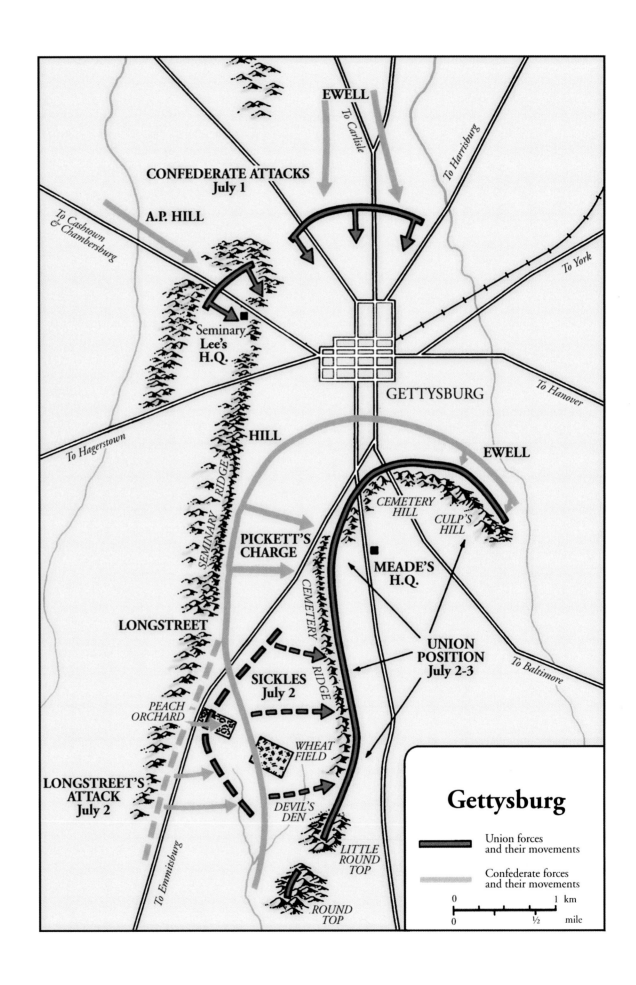

EWELL

To Carlisle

To Harrisburg

CONFEDERATE ATTACKS
July 1

A.P. HILL

To Cashtown & Chambersburg

To York

Seminary
Lee's
H.Q.

GETTYSBURG

To Hagerstown

HILL

EWELL

To Hanover

CEMETERY
HILL

CULP'S
HILL

PICKETT'S
CHARGE

CEMETERY RIDGE

MEADE'S
H.Q.

SEMINARY RIDGE

LONGSTREET

UNION
POSITION
July 2-3

To Baltimore

SICKLES
July 2

PEACH
ORCHARD

WHEAT
FIELD

LONGSTREET'S
ATTACK
July 2

DEVIL'S
DEN

Gettysburg

To Emmitsburg

LITTLE
ROUND
TOP

Union forces
and their movements

Confederate forces
and their movements

ROUND
TOP

0   1 km

0   ½   mile

corps was not fully on the field at sunrise. Lee had hoped for an early-morning attack. After he issued a direct order for an assault in midmorning on July 2, Longstreet exhibited a running display of complaints, alternate proposals, and foot dragging that extended into the afternoon.

In addition, the Union flank was not where Lee thought it was. Fighting took place on the Federal center and right. It was inconclusive owing to bad coordination. Midafternoon was passing when Longstreet finally unleashed his attack. Confederates bumped into Federals who had advanced off the high ground. Then ensued what Longstreet would later term "the best three hours' fighting ever done by any troops on any battlefield."

Devil's Den, the Peach Orchard, and the Wheatfield all became swathed in blood as men charged headlong and struggled violently for possession of small plots of ground. Late in the afternoon, Confederates reached Little Round Top. They swarmed toward the heights and control of the vital ridge. Col. Joshua Chamberlain and his Twentieth Maine held fast until their ammunition was exhausted. Then Chamberlain ordered an unorthodox but now famous bayonet charge. The Union colonel spoke for both sides when he later observed: "The two lines met and broke and mingled in the shock. The crash of musketry gave way to cuts and thrusts. How men held on, each one knows—not I. But manhood commands admiration." Chamberlain's isolated assault crumbled the momentum of the Confederate attack and saved Little Round Top.

Nightfall came, and the screams of the wounded replaced the sound of the guns. Both armies stood intact and bloodied. Lee had won the first day, Meade the second. The outcome of the struggle was still in doubt. That evening Jeb Stuart

rejoined the army. Lee greeted him with icy severity: "Well, General Stuart, you are here at last."

With Longstreet still remonstrating, Lee stated his determination to continue his attacks. Two days of action against the flanks had been nonproductive. By deduction, the weak point must be the Union center. That would be the prime target tomorrow.

Again Lee assigned Longstreet to direct the assault. It would seem that the cumulative strain of the campaign had dulled Lee's senses, for he was entrusting the climactic effort to an officer whose recalcitrance had been consistent since the army prepared to leave Virginia. Yet the other

Joshua L. Chamberlain (1828–1914) was one of the more improbable heroes of the war. A New England minister and college professor who practically sneaked off to war in 1862, he would participate in twenty-four engagements and survive six battle wounds. Promotion to general and the Congressional Medal of Honor were among the honors he received.

THE U.S. MODEL 1855 RIFLE, ALSO KNOWN
AS THE HARPERS FERRY RIFLE

Half of the Twentieth Maine
had fallen, ammunition was
gone, and Confederates were
sweeping toward them. A
desperate Col. Joshua
Chamberlain ordered his
New Englanders to fix bayonets and charge. The unexpected assault broke the
Southern line and saved the
Union left flank at Little
Round Top.

two corps commanders were new. Additionally, Powell Hill was sick, with his corps strangely scattered. Ewell's corps was far on the left flank. It would make a secondary attack. Maj. Gen. George E. Pickett's Virginia division, reinforced by Gen. Johnston Pettigrew's North Carolina division and other troops, would form the principal strike force of about fifteen thousand men.

Poor timing by the Confederates throughout July 3 marked the fighting. Lee apparently expected all of the action to begin around dawn. Ewell launched his distracting assault at sunrise against Culp's Hill. The attack was piecemeal, and it ended in failure hours before Longstreet got his men into position.

A hot sun made the afternoon bright and uncomfortable. The two sides waged an intense, ninety-minute artillery duel. Near 3 P.M. an apprehensive silence fell over the land. The most dramatic moment in American military history had arrived.

Mile-long waves of Confederates with the precision of a parade emerged from the woods and started across fourteen hundred yards of open ground toward Cemetery Ridge and the Union army. Battle flags fluttered above the soldiers. Sunlight glinted from musket barrels. Here and there a band played.

The Southerners did not, as later writers claimed, remain perfectly aligned. Farmers, clerks, students, fishermen, mountaineers—all being shot at by thousands of enemy soldiers—could hardly be expected to advance across three-quarters of a mile of rough ground, scale four fences, and retain throughout it all any kind of symmetrical order. Nevertheless, in the words of one commentator, the spectacle was "the climax of the ante-bellum South in its archaic gallantry."

More than two hundred Federal cannon opened with explosive shells, then switched to canister as the Confederates drew nearer. Union infantry poured volley after volley of musketry into the approaching gray ranks. Gaping holes appeared in the columns. Men dutifully dressed their lines as comrades fell around them. Soon no alignment

For a week Lee had been groping blindly into Pennsylvania. Two days of intense fighting had occurred at Gettysburg, and still the whereabouts of Stuart and his roving cavalry—the eyes of the army—were unknown to Lee. On the night of July 2, Stuart finally arrived at army headquarters. Lee greeted him with momentary exasperation but still retained complete faith in his chief of cavalry.

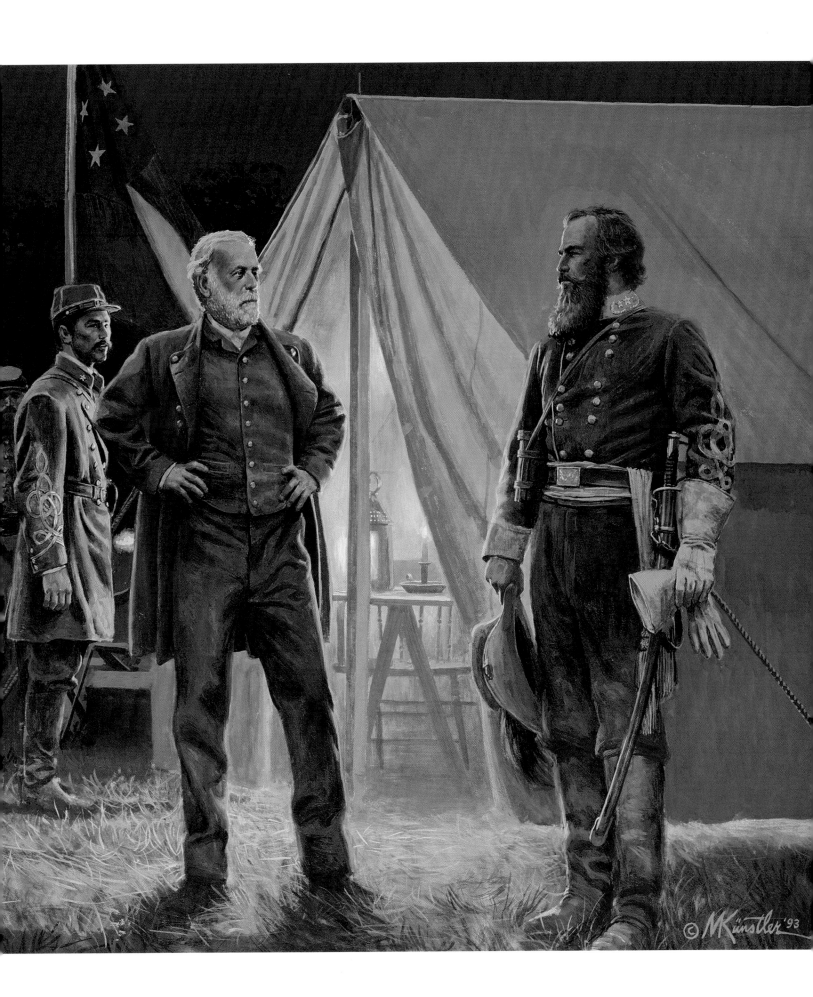

Longstreet was bluff and self-assertive. When not in agreement with announced strategy—as was the case at Gettysburg—he argued and sulked. Lee treated the burly general with far greater patience than most commanders would have done. Longstreet's greatest moments were at Antietam, Fredericksburg, Chickamauga, and the Wilderness. Gettysburg was his worst performance.

In midafternoon that Friday, July 3, 1863, ragged Confederates emerged from the woods and began a charge that would take them to defeat but carry them into legend in the process. Among the units in Gen. George Pickett's division was the brigade of Gen. Lewis Armistead. He followed tradition by leading his soldiers forward and holding his hat aloft so that they could rally on him in the smoke and confusion.

OVERLEAF:

Brig. Gen. Lewis A. Armistead led a Virginia brigade in that terrible July 3 attack at Gettysburg. Armistead was a widower, a warm-hearted professional soldier whose paternalistic spirit led soldiers to refer to him admiringly as "the old man." He died inside the Union lines that day, mortally wounded by soldiers under his close friend of prewar days, Gen. Winfield S. Hancock.

existed. Confederates gathered in little bunches and continued to press toward Cemetery Ridge.

One handful of 150 men, led by Gen. Lewis A. Armistead, actually reached the Union position. They clambered over a stone wall, advanced forty yards into the Union lines, and then broke apart under a fire from three directions. Armistead clung to a cannon as he slumped mortally wounded to the ground.

The Pickett-Pettigrew assault failed because it was impossible to succeed. "We gained nothing but glory," a Virginia captain exclaimed, "and lost our bravest men." The charging columns had been torn to pieces. More than seven thousand Southerners fell in a battle that lasted barely an hour. In Pickett's division, every officer save one above the rank of major was a casualty.

Survivors stumbled back to the Confederate lines in shock. Gen. Cadmus Wilcox reported to Lee and sought to tell him of the losses. Wilcox choked, then began sobbing. Lee touched his shoulder in sympathy. "Never mind, General," he said gently, "all this has been my fault. It is *I* who have lost this fight, and you must help me out of it the best way you can."

With that, Lee began riding up and down the line to give personal reassurances as beaten men came back into the woods. They were no longer invincible, but they were still his beloved soldiers.

Three days of fighting at Gettysburg came to an end with that Confederate repulse. Losses were staggering. Meade's 23,000 casualties included 3,100 dead. Some 28,000 Southerners, a third of Lee's army, had been killed, wounded, or captured. Seventeen of fifty-two Confederate generals were gone.

It was an attack doomed from the beginning. Some fifteen thousand Southerners swept across an open expanse three-quarters of a mile wide in an assault against highly fortified Union lines on Cemetery Ridge at Gettysburg. Confederate gallantry and Federal valor merged in a massive arena of death, smoke, and noise that prevailed for an hour. To men on both sides who survived it, Pickett's Charge was the climax of their lives.

Confederate survivors staggered back to their lines after the July 3 assault and found their commander waiting for them. Lee's greatest concern at the moment, an artillery captain noted, "seemed to be to break the shock of the repulse . . . and probably it was this, coupled with his great magnanimity, that led him to say . . . 'It is all my fault.'"

For the Army of Northern Virginia, the trip home was a nightmare. Stunning defeat hung heavily over the slowly moving column. Pouring rain added to the misery. The hospital train consisted of a file of blood-spattered wagons seven miles long. Meade's heavily bruised forces shied away from an effective pursuit. Both armies had been traumatized by the events at Gettysburg.

It was clear now that the loss of Jackson marked a pronounced line of demarcation in the annals of the Army of Northern Virginia. Delegation of authority, under loose orders that encouraged a wide degree of latitude in their execution, had been the basis for Lee's great triumphs during the ten months that Jackson was with him. Yet at Gettysburg, with the lieutenant only seven weeks in the grave, the system failed Lee. He tried to do it all himself, and it did not work. He had no great tactician of first-class ability to drive unswervingly toward victory. As many writers have concluded, the price of success at Chancellorsville was the cost of defeat at Gettysburg.

Lee returned to Virginia with an enemy in no mood to launch a new offensive against Richmond. Inside the capital, however, disappointment turned to open criticism of Lee's generalship in Pennsylvania. A month after the battle, Lee asked President Davis to relieve him of command in favor of "a younger and abler man." Lee wrote: "I am alone to blame. I cannot accomplish what I myself desire. How can I fulfill the expectations of others?"

Davis, of course, would hear nothing about a resignation. Lee was the bedrock of Southern hopes. He must remain the leader of the army and concentrate his energies on defending Virginia. Declining strength played a role, to be sure, but because no Jackson stood in the wings ready to implement Lee's daring, the conduct of the Confederate army changed markedly. Lee never again attempted the spectacular dividing of his army that he had risked five times when Jackson was with him. Lee would now have to wage a defensive war—a slugging match that he could

AT LEFT:
Retreat presses hardest on the commanding general. Losing a battle carries more than a personal stigma; the army chief must bear the burden of his soldiers dead and badly injured. A withdrawal in the rain, with screams coming from untold numbers of wounded men piled into springless wagons, would have burned the heart of any man of feelings—especially a person of Lee's temperament.

OVERLEAF:
Civil War armies usually did not fight in wintertime. Yet for ill-equipped, hungry, and homesick soldiers, the cold months tried their souls. Some found a measure of contentment during the Christmas season through the relatively new American custom of having a yuletide tree. It reassured their hopes of "peace on earth, good will to men."

and let us say no more about it." Hill would become Lee's most dependable general during the last year of the war, but at this point Lee was feeling the strain of defeat and illness.

Winter came, and the army went into encampment south of the Rapidan River. Four months of hardship followed as emaciated soldiers in rags sought food and clothing. Lee was painfully aware of the suffering. To his army he issued a proclamation that stated in part: "Soldiers! You tread with no unequal step the road by which your fathers marched through . . . privations . . . to independence. Continue to emulate in the future, as you have in the past, their valor in arms, their patient endurance of hardships . . . and be assured that the just God who crowned their efforts with success will, in His own good time, send down His blessing upon yours."

A commander who spoke in that spirit to his men was bound to have their affection. Lee never seemed to realize the devotion his soldiers had for him. An example of such feeling had occurred in one of the battles that year. A young Confederate started to the rear with a shattered right arm. Lee saw him. "I grieve for you, my poor fellow," he said. "Can I do anything for you?"

"Yes, sir," came the reply. "You can shake hands with me, General, if you will consent to take my left hand."

Lee's eyes filled with tears as he silently grasped the private's extended hand with both of his own.

The Union general who stood tallest at the end of the Civil War was Ulysses S. Grant (1822–85), the architect of Northern victory. Shy, with a beard cropped closely and in the plainest of uniforms, Grant was aggressive and unyielding. A Confederate general warned of him in 1864, "That man will fight us every day and every hour until the end of the war."

not win. Still, he was a soldier and a Virginian. He would do his duty to the end.

Opposing armies again settled into positions in northern Virginia. In October, Lee heard that Meade had transferred two corps to duty in Tennessee. This convinced Lee to strike while the Union army was weak. Yet Meade's line of retreat was shorter than Lee's line of advance. A. P. Hill managed to overtake what he thought was the enemy rear guard at Bristoe Station. In his eagerness to attack on October 14, Hill gave little thought to reconnaissance. Two North Carolina brigades charged into the center of an L-shaped position manned by two Federal corps. The forty-minute fight produced fourteen hundred Confederate casualties.

The day following this action, Lee rode over the field covered with dead soldiers and listened as Hill tried to explain what had gone wrong. The commander's patience ran short. "Well, well, General," he interrupted, "bury those poor men

UNION DRUM

[142]

War resumed in May 1864 with Lee facing yet another opponent. In March, President Lincoln had promoted Gen. U. S. Grant to the resurrected grade of lieutenant general (a rank that only George Washington had previously held) and assigned him as general in chief of all Union army forces. Grant wished to stay removed from the political pressures of Washington. He therefore opted to make his headquarters with the Army of the Potomac. After all, the Virginia theater of operations was the war's show window.

Meade would continue to lead the Army of the Potomac, with Grant looking over his shoulder. In truth, Grant took control of the army. Virginia was where the war would be won or lost. The Army of the Potomac was the North's major instrument, the Gray Fox still the primary target.

Grant hardly looked the part of a soldier who could defeat Lee. He had drank too heavily in the "old" army and a failure in civilian life. Short, spare, somewhat unkempt, a cigar close at hand, he never seemed to have much to say. He had won a number of victories in the West, including a successful envelopment of the key Mississippi River fortress of Vicksburg. Now, in the war's third spring, he came east. He arrived without nickname or striking pose or desire to impress anyone. What he brought with him was a reputation as an unemotional slugger: a fighter with single-minded aggressiveness and bulldog determination.

The plan that Grant developed for the 1864 campaign was typical of the man. Concerted attacks would take place on all fronts, with enemy armies rather than enemy territory the targets. Anything associated with the Southern war effort must be neutralized. Generals in the past had pursued war as a game of chess. Grant would now play checkers.

Some Union officers, ready to admit that the greatest general in the war was Lee, were skeptical of the new general in chief. "Well, Grant has never met Bobby Lee and his boys yet," one declared. True, but Lee had never before confronted Grant. The new Federal commander made his intentions clear. "Lee's army will be your first objective point," he told Meade. "Wherever Lee goes, there you will go also."

The two adversaries were at full strength as trees began to leaf with the coming of spring. A repaired and replenished Federal army numbered 120,000 soldiers. Lee was confident of the

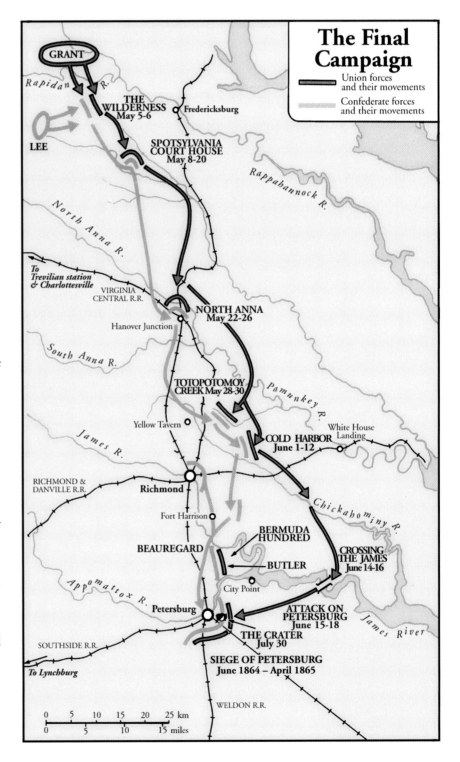

Fierce combat in the Wilderness on May 5–6, 1864, brought the Union army's new advance on Richmond to a halt. The new commanding general, Grant, viewed the Wilderness as the beginning of the end of Lee's army. In the darkness of May 6–7, with Gen. George G. Meade by his side, Grant disdained withdrawal and resumed the southward advance. The Army of the Potomac would not retreat again.

prowess of his army, even though he could put no more than 65,000 lean and taut men in the field.

Late in April, Longstreet's corps returned from assignment in the West. Lee rode over to review the troops, who made every effort to be impressive in appearance. One of them stated: "General Lee must have felt good in getting the welcome extended to him. . . . The men hung around him and seemed satisfied to lay their hands on his gray horse or touch the bridle, or the stirrup, or the old General's leg—anything that Lee had was sacred to us fellows who had just come back. And the General—he could not help from breaking down . . . tears traced down his cheeks."

Confederate soldiers remained convinced that they could beat any Yankees on their home ground. Civilian spirits were falsely high as well. Officials in Richmond still expected Lee to produce miracles without support or supplies.

Union forces in the first days of May began to drive into Virginia from three directions. One column entered the Shenandoah Valley to destroy Lee's food base and secure the western flank of operations. The newly created Army of the James started up the south bank of the river for which it was named. Its purpose was to threaten Petersburg and Richmond. Grant with the Army of the Potomac would cross the Rapidan and advance through the Wilderness.

Northern newspapers continued to chant: "On to Richmond!" Yet the Southern capital was not to be Grant's goal. He would of necessity move in that direction because Lee's army had to defend the city at all costs. Once Grant made contact with the Confederate army, he would hold fast and fight hard. Sooner or later, superiority in numbers would prevail. The Union army would defeat Lee and end the war. With that scenario established, Grant led the North's largest fighting force across the Rapidan.

Lee knew of the three-pronged Federal offensive. He found himself actually defending against an encirclement in his own state. Once again Lee reacted unpredictably. Among his characteristics

wounded men burned to death, and tree smoke mingled with gun smoke created a choking gloom all over the Wilderness. Nightfall came with the armies still locked in combat. Both commanders knew that the battle must continue. Only yards separated opposing lines through the hours of darkness.

Federals banked in three corps counterattacked at 5 A.M. Ewell's line held, but heavy assaults sent Hill's troops up the road in rapid retreat. If the enemy was not immobilized, the Confederate army could be destroyed. Federals were about to seize Lee's guns in a rare clearing at the Widow Tapp's farm when an anxious Lee turned around and saw a group of Confederates double-timing toward the front. They were the Texans of John B. Hood's brigade in Longstreet's corps. The rest of the Confederate army was coming onto the field!

Lee was so excited that he waved his hat over his head and prepared to lead a charge himself against the oncoming Federals. "Go back, General Lee!" the Texans shouted. "Go back!"

The commander paid them no heed. Now came louder yells: "Lee to the rear! Lee to the rear! We won't go unless you go back!" Those cries, coupled with the arrival of Longstreet and the need for a conference, calmed Lee's agitation.

Longstreet's heavy countercharge rolled the Union advance all the way back to its starting point. That afternoon, in a chilling coincidence, Longstreet was severely wounded by musketry from his own men only yards from where, a year earlier, Jackson had received a similar fire. Lee now had lost his only veteran corps commander in the first battle of the campaign. Meanwhile, the fighting on Ewell's front was a stalemate. Darkness brought an end to the two-day engagement. Grant had lost eighteen thousand men while Lee suffered eleven thousand casualties.

In the past, defeated Union armies had retreated and licked their wounds for a time before starting forward again. Yet this battle was no defeat because Grant refused to admit that it

No one ever accused Gen. John B. Hood (1831–79) of being hesitant to fight. A young bearded giant from Kentucky, he commanded the famous Texas Brigade because his native state was neutral in the war. Hood received a permanently crippled arm at Gettysburg and lost a leg at Chickamauga. Army command in 1864 proved to be beyond his ability.

was an unwillingness to fight where his opponent wanted him to fight. He preferred to choose his own field, and he did so now. The tangled confusion of the Wilderness was no place to do battle, but an outnumbered and outgunned Lee was not going to wait for the enemy to move into open country where it could maneuver fully. Lee sent a call for Longstreet's right wing of the army to join him quickly from Gordonsville; then, with the corps of Ewell and Hill on parallel routes, Lee drove into the Federal flank as Grant's army advanced south through the Wilderness on the Brock road.

Fighting began on the morning of May 5 and continued unabated through the day. Two separate battles, hardly three miles apart, took place for control of road intersections. Men came under heavy fire from enemies they could not see in the thick timber. Woods caught fire, helpless

was a defeat. He ordered the Union army to resume its southward advance. The objective was still to turn Lee's right flank and force him away from Richmond. Lee had sensed that design. Both armies began a race for the next important point: the crossroads at Spotsylvania. The Confederates won by the slim distance of a few rods.

While Grant stabbed at Lee's position, the Confederate general constructed five miles of formidable entrenchments. At one point Lee's line was in a horseshoe shape to guard a principal road crossing. Grant regarded that sector as the weak point in the Confederate defenses. Shortly after daylight on a rainy May 12, Federals made a massive assault against the west face of the salient.

Some of the most savage fighting of the Civil War ensued that Thursday. Johnny Rebs and Billy Yanks fought, fell, killed, and died for the better part of seventeen hours. Only the width of the earthworks divided the two armies. Lee's lines bent but held. When night came, corpses lay five deep in the mud. Some of the bodies had been reduced by repeated fire to torn bits of rag and bone. Union killed and wounded were seven thousand, Confederate losses were higher, and all of this had taken place around trenches no more than a quarter-mile in length. Thereafter, the salient would be remembered as the Bloody Angle.

Grant was undeterred by the high losses he incurred in the first week of the Virginia campaign. He told the Union War Department that he proposed to "fight it out on this line if it takes all summer."

Lee's health was precarious at the time. His spirits received a stern blow with news of another personal loss. On May 11, on the outskirts of Richmond, Jeb Stuart and his cavalry engaged a heavy force of Union horsemen. Stuart was mortally wounded in the action. Lee accepted the news by stating: "He never brought me a piece of false information." To Mrs. Lee he wrote: "A more zealous, ardent, brave and devoted soldier than Stuart the Confederacy cannot have."

A somber Lee grew realistic about the dark turn of the war that spring. His army was resisting destruction, and it was inflicting terrible casualties on its opponent, but Lee's forces had lost their old capacity to seize the initiative and turn a stubborn defense into a brilliant offense. The Army of Northern Virginia was not losing, but it was not winning either. If the Confederate States of America were to remain alive, Lee's army had to win.

At an informal council of war during the twelve days of operations around Spotsylvania, one of Lee's generals made reference to Grant's senseless and bloody attacks. Lee took exception. "Gentlemen, I think General Grant has managed his affairs remarkably well up to the present time." A few moments later, Lee voiced an opinion shared fully by Grant. The Confederate army cannot endure a siege, Lee observed. "We must end this business on the battlefield, not in a fortified place."

Persistently, Grant moved again toward the Southern right flank. Illness, strain, and the hard physical life were bearing down on Lee. He missed the slashing attacks of Jackson and the stubborn dependability of Longstreet. Ewell was fading as a corps commander. Powell Hill was unknowingly in the first throes of a fatal kidney

THE HAVERSACK OF
CAPT. O. JENNINGS WISE OF THE
FORTY-SIXTH VIRGINIA INFANTRY

disorder and not always up to high performance. More and more, the proud Confederate force was becoming a one-man army, reverting back to the loose organization of divisions that Lee had inherited two years before.

Confederates managed to block Grant at the North Anna River. The Union army again sidled to the east. It crossed the Pamunkey River but came upon Lee's army waiting in battle line at Cold Harbor. This crossroads was in the battle area where Lee in 1862 had first emerged as a field commander. At Cold Harbor, Grant either lost his patience or became deluded by understatements of Lee's strength. The Union general ordered a concentrated frontal assault against fieldworks supervised by an adversary who was one of the army's most talented engineers.

Many of the Federal soldiers were convinced beforehand of the futility of the attack they had to make. During the night of waiting, some men wrote their names and units on pieces of paper and pinned them on their shirts for easier identification later by the burial details. A New England soldier made a final entry in his diary: "June 3, Cold Harbor. I was killed." The June 3 action barely lasted an hour. More than seven thousand Union soldiers fell. It was Grant's worst mistake of the war.

His army reeled in defeat, but Lee's ranks were too thin in numbers and worn in bodies to press their advantage. Even if they could have made a counterattack, there was no one capable of leading them. Lee could only stand firm and wait to see what Grant would do next.

Cold Harbor marked the end of a month that had witnessed the most sustained combat of the war. The two armies had never been out of contact. Grant had hammered, Lee had countered. While the Union general swung a broadax, the Southern commander used a saber. Army formations had been wrecked.

Grant had sustained 55,000 casualties—an average of 2,000 men lost per day. Northern editors and politicians were calling him "the butcher." However, Lee's losses were in excess of 32,000 men, and while Grant could fill his gaps

No battle of the Civil War equaled the May 12 contest at Spotsylvania for contempt of death and immeasurable ferocity. Men struggled in rain, fog, and mud. Fighting raged along a lone breastwork; dead men fell atop wounded men as neither side budged. One veteran soldier called the battle "the most terrible twenty-four hours of our service in the war."

On May 15, 1864, Federal
Gen. Franz Sigel's advance up
the Shenandoah Valley came to
an abrupt halt at New Market. A hodgepodge force of five
thousand Confederates under
former U.S. Vice President
John C. Breckinridge attacked
in the rain and broke the
Union line. A key element in
the victorious assault was the
corps of teenaged cadets from
the Virginia Military Institute, where Jackson had taught
for ten years.

from the huge manpower base in the North, Lee could not replace his killed and wounded. It was now a war of attrition: of force against force involving the wearing down of one side by its numerically superior foe.

Union efforts elsewhere in Virginia that spring suffered inglorious setbacks. Gen. Franz Sigel's small army pressed into the Valley of Virginia to destroy the Confederate granary and avenue of attack. Sigel got as far as New Market. On a rainy May 15, a hodgepodge Confederate force under former U.S. Vice President John C. Breckinridge soundly defeated Sigel. In the Confederate assault that day were 241 teenage cadets from the Virginia Military Institute. Ten were killed or mortally injured; forty-nine others were wounded.

The Army of the James, under floundering Gen. Benjamin F. Butler, fared no better. Butler advanced tentatively up the James, received a pounding on May 16 from a small enemy force, and took refuge in a peninsula formed by the confluence of the James and Appomattox Rivers. The Confederates built an entrenched line across the neck of the Union position and effectively corked Butler in a bottle, a disgusted Grant stated. Yet Grant was not finished with his own campaign.

In mid-June, with an unspeakable battle stench filling the hot summer air on the Virginia Peninsula, Grant led the Union army in another wide arc: this time across the James and toward the railroad junction at Petersburg. Securing that point would enable Grant to advance on Richmond's soft underbelly. That in turn would force Lee into open battle.

The Union army failed to achieve its immediate goal. Part of the problem lay with Federal officers and men afflicted with what some called the "Cold Harbor syndrome." They were reluctant to continue making frontal attacks against Lee's entrenchments. Too many soldiers had been "foolishly and wantonly sacrificed" trying to defeat Lee that way, a Union officer declared.

Such Union hesitation enabled Lee to shift his army southward over the James to prevent the loss of Petersburg. Grant, for all of his maneuvering,

War tests the might and the faith of a nation's people. Both show forth in this depiction. On a cold winter night in 1862, Confederate cavalry passed Opequon Presbyterian Church at Kernstown, Virginia, just as the midweek evening worship service was ending. For a moment, war and peace came together as soldiers exchanged looks with civilians.

was still farther from Richmond than McClellan had been two years earlier. Yet Grant and Lee were both cognizant of basic truisms. Lee had foiled Grant's designs, but he had been unable to implement any designs of his own. At Petersburg, Grant had nowhere to go and Lee was too weak to move.

The Richmond-Petersburg line became the principal Virginia arena for the last year of the war. Soldiers eventually faced one another over a thirty-five-mile expanse. Every foot had to be defended. In addition, Lee had to guard his flanks. He could not retreat without falling back into the defenses of Richmond. The rail lines diverging from Petersburg must be kept open. They were the Southern army's lifelines for food and supplies.

From the outset of the campaign six weeks earlier, Lee had followed a single objective. He strove to stand between Grant and Richmond while always maneuvering to make maximum use of his limited forces. Mobility was Lee's greatest asset. Being pinned down into a static defense was

John B. Gordon (1832–1904) was a prewar Georgia attorney, newspaperman, and mine developer. In the first weeks of the conflict, he organized a company of volunteers. Four years later at Appomattox, he was a major general commanding Jackson's old corps. The citizen-soldier later was a U.S. senator, governor, and first commander in chief of the United Confederate Veterans.

his worst fear. At Spotsylvania, he had told his generals with prophetic insight: "We must destroy this army of Grant's before he gets to the James River. If he gets there, it will become a siege, and then it will be a mere question of time."

That dreaded moment had arrived. Lee was immobilized, and Grant held a short chain. Any shift by Lee ran the risk of losing Petersburg or Richmond or one of the rail lines. The war was now to become a siege—precisely the kind of contest that Lee could not hope to win.

Lee stubbornly refused to accept his army's loss of offensive power. His nature as a soldier rebelled against a defensive posture that his own military knowledge warned could have only one end. In the middle of June, Lee employed a diversion quite similar to Jackson's 1862 Valley campaign. The army commander dispatched Gen. Jubal Early and thirteen thousand troops to the Shenandoah.

"Old Jube" Early was no Jackson, but he was a tough soldier who enjoyed a fight. His dual mission was to clear the area of marauding Federals and then to make a threat on Washington. The hope was that this would force Grant to transfer large numbers of troops from the Petersburg front—a move that would give Lee a chance at escape.

Early made a good try. He routed Federals in his front, then turned and advanced to the outskirts of the Union capital. Washington turned out to be too powerfully defended. Early led his men back into the Valley, where the besieger soon found himself besieged.

Grant was weary of repeated contests for control of the Shenandoah Valley. He thereupon sent one of his best lieutenants, wiry little Philip H. Sheridan, to secure the region once and for all. Grant told Sheridan to take forty thousand veteran soldiers and to leave the Valley "a barren waste" so that "crows flying over it . . . will have to carry their provender with them."

Sheridan carried out his assignment literally. Outnumbering Early by almost three to one, he gained battle victories at Winchester, Fisher's

Hill, and Cedar Creek in the space of a month. This eliminated any further Confederate resistance. Federal soldiers then turned their attention to burning barns, destroying crops, and slaughtering livestock. What was left of the Shenandoah Valley became the property of the Union army. Lee had lost his breadbasket.

The great siege at Richmond and Petersburg lasted ten months. Each side constructed elaborate breastworks that zigzagged as far as the eye could see. In September, Grant attempted a knockout blow. The Army of the Potomac struck both ends of Lee's line simultaneously. Federals managed to capture Fort Harrison in the Richmond works, but they were unable to effect a breakthrough there or at Petersburg. At the end of October, Grant made a heavy attack on the southern end of the line. Lee's gaunt veterans waged a heroic struggle and drove back the Federals with heavy losses.

All the while, Grant slowly extended his line farther to the southwest to cut the railroads that the South had to have to preserve Richmond. With constantly dwindling resources, Lee was compelled to stretch his own lines in response. His army was less than half the size of Grant's. The stretching process could not continue indefinitely. At some point the taut Confederate line would snap.

Weeks passed, skirmishes occurred daily, casualties mounted. Disease and desertion plagued the skeletal army under Lee. The coldest winter of the war wreaked havoc with men in rags. Yet shivering and starving Confederates proudly endured, styling themselves in the process as "Lee's Miserables."

As command problems bore heavily on Lee, so did physical maladies. Repeated colds, neuralgia, and occasional diarrhea aggravated an ongoing heart condition. At one point the aging general complained that surgeons "have been tapping me all over like a steam boiler before condemning it." His health became somewhat erratic. Periods of pain alternated with times of relative comfort. Yet Lee was always tired.

THE VMI MEDAL AWARDED AFTER THE WAR TO VMI CADETS WHO HAD FOUGHT AT THE BATTLE OF NEW MARKET

His February 6 appointment as general in chief of all Confederate armies was a meaningless gesture. Lee remained in the field with his army for the simple reason that little remained of the Confederacy except what Lee was defending. A member of his staff wrote that winter: "Such was the love and veneration of the men for him that they came to look upon the cause as General Lee's cause, and they fought for it because they loved him. To them he represented cause, country, and all."

The end of winter found Grant's 124,000 well-equipped soldiers poised for action. Lee's once fearsome units had diminished to no more than a collection of sick and half-starved ragamuffins clinging to their battle flags. On March 25, Lee tried to force an escape route with a surprise attack on the Union center at Fort Stedman. It failed. Grant marked time for a few days. Then he struck. Some 53,000 Federals broke the Confederate right flank at Five Forks. The heaviest bombardment of the war followed that night as Federal cannon rained shells along the Petersburg front.

With dawn, April 2, came a full-scale attack by Grant's army. Among the first Confederates killed was Gen. A. P. Hill. Fighting raged through the day. Waves of Union soldiers overran long stretches of Lee's fieldworks. The Southern commander had no choice now but to abandon

Petersburg, as well as Richmond, and retreat with his army to a position somewhere to the west.

For five days Lee's army struggled toward an unknown haven. Early in the retreat an artillerist got a close look at the man affectionately called Marse Robert. Lee's face "was still calm, as it always was, but his carriage was no longer erect. . . . The troubles of those days had already plowed great furrows in his forehead. His eyes were red; his cheeks sunken and haggard; his face colorless. No one who looked upon him then . . . can ever forget the intense agony written upon those features."

Grant's forces pushed furiously in pursuit. The campaign resembled an old animal with a pack of wolves closing in on it. Union cavalry kept getting across Lee's line of march, Union infantry were on his flanks, and Grant with the major part of the army was pressing on Lee's rear. No more than half of the Confederates were armed or in fighting condition. The rest were exhausted soldiers who followed Lee, impelled by some blind glory of the human soul.

It all ended at Appomattox Court House with Lee's soldiers hopelessly surrounded. The Army of Northern Virginia had given the Southern nation the only hope of independence and growth it had ever had; its leader had been the principal inspiration of the Confederacy for three years. Now it was Palm Sunday, and Appomattox marked the end of the road.

Lee could have disdained surrender. He could have ordered his army to disperse, every man for himself, waging guerrilla warfare for as long as it

In a supreme effort to regain control of the lower Shenandoah Valley, a ragged Confederate army launched a surprise attack on October 19, 1864, at Cedar Creek. Union forces at and around Belle Grove plantation bolted to the rear. Confederate Gen. John B. Gordon sought to exploit the moment, but heavy Federal counterattacks turned the sunrise of that day into a sunset for the Confederacy in the Valley.

took for the South to be left alone. Such a move would have been natural because civil wars so often degenerate to that level. However, bushwhacker tactics would not bring the South victory; they could easily bring the South annihilation. Lee would have none of it. The Southern states had waged an honorable contest. Just as honorably must the Southern states accept defeat.

So the tired but dignified Virginian met Grant inside the Union lines and agreed to generous terms of surrender. The dramatic scene in the front parlor of Wilmer McLean's home was one of those rare moments in history when the vanquished commanded more attention than the victor.

On April 6, 1865, Federal infantry and cavalry struck the rear of Lee's retreating army at Sayler's Creek. The action cost Lee seventy-five hundred casualties as well as most of his wagon train. When Lee reached the scene, he took a battle flag and held it aloft as a rallying point for soldiers who flocked around him with a mixture of relief and exhaustion.

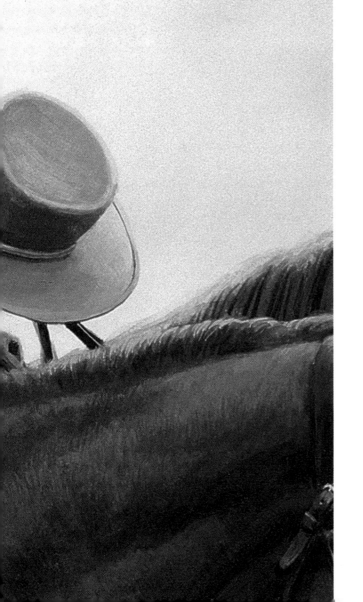

PART

*Defeat
to
Victory*

DEFEAT TO VICTORY

TRAVELLER BORE LEE SLOWLY BACK to his own lines that afternoon. The general stared unseeing at the ground, his heart aching from the realization of defeat. Then "occurred a display of deep feeling on the part of large bodies of men which I suppose has rarely been equalled in history," a Confederate officer wrote.

When they saw the well-known figure of General Lee approaching, there was a general rush from each side of the road to greet him as he passed, and two solid walls of men were formed along the whole distance. . . . As soon as he entered this avenue of those old soldiers— the flower of his army, wild heartfelt cheers arose which so touched General Lee that tears filled his eyes and trickled down his cheeks. . . .

This exhibition of feeling on his part found quick response from the men whose cheers changed to choking sobs as with streaming eyes and many cries of affection they waved their hats as he passed. Each group began in the same way with cheers and ended in the same way with sobs, all the way to his quarters. Grim-bearded men threw themselves on the ground, covered their faces with their hands, and wept like children. Officers of all ranks made no attempt to conceal their feelings, but sat on their horses and sobbed aloud.

A dirt-crusted soldier embodied the broken heart of the Confederacy when he reached out his arms and shouted: "I love you just as well as ever, General Lee!"

The commander had one more duty to fulfill. On April 10, Lee issued General Orders No. 9 to his troops. He praised their "four years of arduous service marked by unsurpassed courage and fortitude." For the sake of those "brave survivors of so many hard fought battles, who have remained steadfast to the last," Lee had determined to surrender. "With an unceasing admiration for your constancy and devotion to your Country, and grateful remembrance of your kind and generous consideration of myself, I bid you all an affectionate farewell. . . . You will take with you the satisfaction that proceeds from the consciousness of duty faithfully performed; and I earnestly pray that a Merciful God will extend to you His blessing and protection." Thus, in the last indomitable act of his military career, Lee ordered his army into history.

Several weeks after Appomattox, a despondent Lee told his wife: "Life is indeed gliding away, and I have nothing good to show for mine that is past. I pray that I may be spared to accomplish something for the benefit of mankind and the honor of God."

Lee *did* accomplish one more thing, and in some respects it was the hallmark of his life. In Stonewall Jackson's adopted town of Lexington was impoverished Washington College. Its forty students and four faculty badly needed a president. In the autumn of 1865, Lee agreed to take charge of the school.

There was no need for the old warrior to become involved in the struggles of postwar education. Nevertheless, Lee brought to the college presidency the same ability and devotion to duty that had marked his army years. He spent his remaining energies in training young men—as well as their parents—to learn from the past and to look to the future.

Under Lee's brief leadership, Washington College's enrollment increased tenfold, its faculty twentyfold. The curriculum established a balance between classical studies of bygone years and the scientific, practical education a war-torn South desperately needed. Lee introduced elective courses and other new features. He personally reviewed

In Lee's final years, some of his afternoon rides in Lexington took him to Jackson's grave. There he remembered the devoted compatriot with whom he had enjoyed so close and successful a relationship. If Lee also pondered the might-have-beens of the war, they were fleeting thoughts. Like Jackson, Lee dutifully accepted life as God had willed it. The good soldier and the good Christian were one.

the progress of each student like a father watching over his son. He revamped the many rules of the college into one axiom: a student should always conduct himself as a gentleman. The school remained Washington College for a number of years, but to untold numbers of people it was "General Lee's College."

In the aftermath of Confederate defeat, Lee became a Southern icon. Yet he shunned large gatherings and public adulation. He refused to write his memoirs or to engage in the war of words that followed the silencing of the guns. Lee granted few interviews and shied away from refighting battles. A favorite pastime was to mount his gray stallion Traveller for a quiet afternoon ride through the countryside. Doubtless those outings took him on occasion to the Lexington cemetery. There Lee stood beside the simple gravestone of his incomparable lieutenant, Jackson, and pondered both the accomplishments and the might-have-beens of their association together.

Cardiovascular problems inevitably grew worse. Lee prepared for the end. In the spring of 1870, he made a southern trip ostensibly for his health. It was a farewell tour. That summer he agreed reluctantly to sit for a portrait and pose for a statue. He died October 12, 1870, following a stroke. A multitude not seen in Lexington since the burial of Jackson attended Lee's funeral and interment in the college chapel. Tributes poured into Lexington from North and South alike. Julia Ward Howe, who had inspired Union soldiers with the stirring words of "The Battle Hymn of the Republic," wrote of Lee:

> A gallant foeman in the fight,
> A brother when the fight was done;
> And so, thy soldier grave beside,
> We honor thee, Virginia's son.

Perhaps former Confederate Gen. Jubal Early best expressed the feelings of the southern people: "Whoever will undertake to draw a parallel between General Lee and his great lieutenant, for the purpose of depreciating the one or the other, cannot have formed the remotest conception of the true character of either of those illustrious men and congenial Christian heroes. Let us be thankful that our cause had two such champions, and that, in their characters, we can furnish the world at large with the best assurance of the principles for which they . . . fought. When asked for our vindication [as southerners], I can triumphantly point to the graves of Lee and Jackson—and look the world squarely in the face."

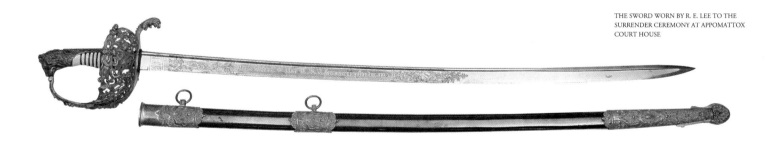

THE SWORD WORN BY R. E. LEE TO THE SURRENDER CEREMONY AT APPOMATTOX COURT HOUSE

THE IMAGES

Jackson (Page 1)
1994
Charcoal
23 x 18 inches
Collection: Hammer Galleries

Lee (Page 1)
1994
Charcoal
23 x 18 inches
Collection: Hammer Galleries

The Angle (Page 6)
Gettysburg, July 3, 1863
1988
Oil on canvas
18 x 24 inches
Collection: Mr. Edward F. Arrigoni

The High Tide (Page 8)
Gettysburg, July 3, 1863
1993
Gouache
16 x 28¾ inches
Collection: Mr. and Mrs. George Kellner

Jefferson Davis (Page 10)
President, Confederate States
1990
Oil on board
10 x 11½ inches
Collection: Dr. Gary LeFleur

Abraham Lincoln
(Page 11)
President, United States
1991
Oil on board
10 x 11⅜ inches
Collection:
Hammer Galleries

Gen. Robert E. Lee
(Page 14)
1991
Oil on board
10 x 11½ inches
Collection:
Dr. Gary LeFleur

"The Enemy Is There!"
(Pages 12–13, 16)
General Lee and Staff,
Gettysburg
1993
Gouache
17 x 13⅝ inches
Collection:
Mr. Robert Cheeley

The Virginia Gentleman
(Page 17)
Gen. Robert E. Lee
1993
Mixed media
16 x 10 inches
Collection:
Mr. Greg Pennington

Lee on Traveller (Page 18)
1995
Mixed media
18½ x 25½ inches
Collection: Hammer Galleries

The Great Decision (Page 20)
Robert E. Lee, April 1861
1995
Mixed media
24¼ x 18½ inches
Collection: Hammer Galleries

The Loneliness of Command
(Pages 22–23)
Gen. Robert E. Lee
1995
Mixed media
18½ x 22½ inches
Collection: Hammer Galleries

The Passing of Command (Pages 24–25)
President Davis and General Lee, May 31, 1862
1995
Mixed media
18½ x 25 inches
Collection: Hammer Galleries

". . . War Is So Terrible"
(Page 32)
Longstreet and Lee, Fredericksburg,
December 13, 1862
1995
Mixed media
23¾ x 18¼ inches
Collection: Hammer Galleries

Maj. Thomas J. Jackson Leaves VMI (Pages 40–41)
Lexington, Virginia, April 21, 1861
1995
Mixed media
17½ x 20¾ inches
Collection: Hammer Galleries

"I Order You Both to the Rear!" (Page 27)
Gen. A. P. Hill, President Davis, General Lee,
June 30, 1862
1995
Mixed media
14 x 22½ inches
Collection: Hammer Galleries

*Gen. Thomas
"Stonewall" Jackson*
(Page 36)
1991
Oil on board
10 x 11½ inches
Collection:
Dr. Gary LeFleur

"Old Jack" (Pages 42–43)
Gen. Stonewall Jackson
1995
Oil on board
14 x 18 inches
Collection: Hammer Galleries

Lee at Fredericksburg
(Pages 28–29)
Princess Anne Street, 9:40 A.M., November 20, 1862
1990
Oil on canvas
34 x 56 inches
Collection: Mr. and Mrs. Michael Sharpe

Stonewall Jackson and Staff
(Page 38)
1995
Gouache
18½ x 15 inches
Collection: Hammer Galleries

"There Stands Jackson Like a Stone Wall"
(Pages 34–35, 44–45)
Gen. Thomas J. Jackson at First Manassas, July 21, 1861
1991
Oil on canvas
24 x 36 inches
Collection: Dr. and Mrs. Barry George

The Virginia Orphan (Page 39)
Gen. Thomas
"Stonewall" Jackson
1995
Mixed media
29½ x 18 inches
Collection: Hammer Galleries

Storm Over Gettysburg (Page 31)
Generals Lee and Longstreet,
July 3, 1863
1993
Gouache
14½ x 12½ inches
Collection: Hammer Galleries

"The Sweetest Music . . ." (Pages 46–47)
Gen. Stonewall Jackson, November 4, 1861
1995
Mixed media
19 x 25 inches
Collection: Hammer Galleries

"Until We Meet Again" (Pages 48–49)
Jackson's Headquarters, Winchester, Virginia, Winter 1862
1990
Oil on canvas
30 x 46 inches
Collection: F&M Bank, Winchester, Virginia

Gen. J. E. B. Stuart (Page 58)
Virginia
1991
Oil on board
10 x 11½ inches
Collection: Dr. Gary LeFleur

"I Will Be Moving Within the Hour" (Pages 64–65)
Second Manassas Campaign, August 1862
1993
Oil on canvas
20 x 40 inches
Collection: American Print Gallery, Gettysburg,
Pennsylvania

Gen. Stonewall Jackson Enters Winchester, Virginia
(Pages 50–51)
May 25, 1862
1988
Oil on canvas
30 x 48 inches
Collection: F&M Bank, Winchester, Virginia

Gen. George McClellan (Page 59)
United States
1990
Oil on board
10 x 11½ inches
Collection: Hammer Galleries

Stuart's Ride Around McClellan (Pages 66–67)
June 13, 1862
1995
Gouache
15¼ x 36 inches
Collection: Hammer Galleries

Jackson on Little Sorrel (Page 53)
1995
Mixed media
18½ x 25½ inches
Collection: Hammer Galleries

Gen. James Longstreet
(Page 68)
South Carolina
1990
Oil on board
10 x 11¼ inches
Collection:
Dr. Gary LeFleur

Model Partnership (Pages 60–61)
Gens. Stonewall Jackson and Robert E. Lee
1995
Mixed media
16 x 23 inches
Collection: Hammer Galleries

Lee's Lieutenants (Page 56)
Generals Jackson, Lee, and Longstreet
1995
Mixed media
18 x 24 inches
Collection: Hammer Galleries

On the Shoulders of Giants (Pages 70–71)
Lee and Jackson, Frayser's Farm, June 30, 1862
1995
Mixed media
18 x 25 inches
Collection: Hammer Galleries

". . . They Were Soldiers Indeed" (Pages 2–3, 62–63, 160–61)
Generals Jackson and Lee, June 28, 1862
1995
Gouache
19½ x 29½ inches
Collection: Hammer Galleries

"President, This Is Our Stonewall Jackson" (Pages 72–73)
Longstreet, Davis, Lee, Stuart, and Jackson, July 2, 1862
1995
Mixed media
18½ x 24 inches
Collection: Hammer Galleries

Stonewall Jackson at Harpers Ferry (Pages 82–83)
September 15, 1862
1992
Oil on canvas
26 x 40 inches
Collection: Mrs. William Bridgeforth

The Scouts of Fredericksburg (Page 93)
Major Von Borcke with Generals Lee and Jackson,
December 12, 1862
1995
Mixed media
17¼ x 24¾ inches
Collection: Hammer Galleries

The Commanders of Manassas (Pages 74–75)
Gens. Longstreet, Lee, and Jackson, August 29, 1862
1995
Mixed media
19 x 23½ inches
Collection: Hammer Galleries

Jackson at Antietam (Pages 86–87)
Gen. Stonewall Jackson, September 18, 1862,
Dunker Church
1989
Oil on canvas
32 x 50 inches
Collection: U.S. Army War College,
Carlisle, Pennsylvania

"Old Jack's" New Uniform (Pages 94–95)
High Command at Fredericksburg, December 12, 1862
1995
Mixed media
18½ x 25½ inches
Collection: Hammer Galleries

Decision at Manassas (Pages 76–77)
Lee, Jackson, and Longstreet, August 29, 1862
1995
Mixed media
18 x 24 inches
Collection: Hammer Galleries

Night Crossing (Pages 88–89)
Lee and Jackson, September 18, 1862
1995
Mixed media
18½ x 25 inches
Collection: Hammer Galleries

The Review at Moss Neck (Pages 54–55, 96–97)
Fredericksburg, Virginia, January 20, 1863
1995
Oil on canvas
24 x 42 inches
Collection: Dr. John Chandler

Reconnaissance at Manassas (Pages 80–81)
Generals Jackson and Lee, August 31, 1862
1995
Mixed media
19 x 26 inches
Collection: Hammer Galleries

Strategy in the Snow (Pages 90–91)
Fredericksburg, Virginia, November 29, 1862
1994
Oil on canvas
27 x 35 inches
Collection: Goldsmith, Agio, Helms and Company

*"And the Two Generals Were
Brought to Tears"* (Page 99)
Jackson and Lee,
Fredericksburg, Virginia,
Spring 1863
1992
Oil on canvas
24 x 20 inches
Collection:
Mr. and Mrs. Frank Gilbreth

The Last Council (Pages 102–3)
Jackson, Lee, and Stuart at Chancellorsville,
May 1, 1863
1990
Oil on canvas
28 x 36 inches
Collection: Arnold and Anne Gumowitz

The Last Meeting (Pages 104–5)
Chancellorsville, May 2, 1863
1994
Oil on canvas
28 x 40 inches
Collection: Hammer Galleries

End of a Legend (Pages 106–7)
Jackson at Chancellorsville, May 2, 1863
1995
Gouache
16½ x 26½ inches
Collection: Hammer Galleries

His Supreme Moment (Pages 108–9)
Lee at Chancellorsville, May 3, 1863
1995
Mixed media
18 x 23¾ inches
Collection: Hammer Galleries

"Oh, I Wish He Was Ours" (Page 114)
Hagerstown, Maryland, June 26, 1863
1991
Oil on canvas
24 x 32 inches
Collection: Mr. and Mrs. Frank B. Gilbreth

Gen. A. P. Hill (Page 116)
C.S.A.
1995
Oil on board
10 x 11¼ inches
Collection: Hammer Galleries

Gen. John Buford (Page 117)
1992
Oil on board
9⅝ x 11 inches
Collection: Hammer Galleries

"Hold at All Cost!" (Pages 118–19)
Gen. John Buford, Gettysburg, July 1, 1863, 9:30 A.M.
1993
Gouache
12½ x 36⅞ inches
Collection: Hammer Galleries

Twilight in Gettysburg (Pages 120–21)
Gen. Robert E. Lee, July 1, 1863
1993
Gouache
16⅜ x 27½ inches
Collection: Hammer Galleries

Gen. Joshua Lawrence Chamberlain
(Page 123)
Maine
1992
Oil on board
9⅝ x 10⅞ inches
Collection: Hammer Galleries

Chamberlain's Charge (Pages 124–25)
Little Round Top, July 2, 1863
1994
Oil on canvas
20 x 32 inches
Collection: Mr. Earl Jones

The Return of Stuart (Pages 126–27)
Generals Lee and Stuart, Gettysburg, July 2, 1863
1993
Gouache
13⅜ x 27½ inches
Collection: Mr. Greg Pennington

Lee's "Old War Horse" (Pages 128–29)
Generals Longstreet and Lee, Gettysburg, Pennsylvania,
July 3, 1863
1993
Gouache
16½ x 27 inches
Collection: Mr. Thomas Taft

"It's All My Fault" (Pages 112–13, 136–37)
Gen. Robert E. Lee at Gettysburg, July 3, 1863
1989
Oil on canvas
26 x 48 inches
Collection: Mr. Thorne Donnelly, Jr.

On to Richmond (Pages 144–45)
Grant in the Wilderness, May 7, 1864
1991
Oil on canvas
30 x 42 inches
Collection: U.S. Army War College,
Carlisle, Pennsylvania

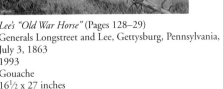

"Steady, Boys, Steady!" (Pages 130–31)
Gen. Lewis A. Armistead, Pickett's Charge, July 3, 1863
1993
Gouache
14 x 37½ inches
Collection: Hammer Galleries

The Long Road South (Pages 138–39)
Fairfield, Pennsylvania, July 4, 1863
1993
Gouache
11⅞ x 17⅞ inches
Collection: Hammer Galleries

Gen. John Bell Hood
(Page 146)
Texas
1991
Oil on board
10 x 11⅜ inches
Collection:
Dr. Gary LeFleur

"Follow Me, Boys!" (Pages 132–33)
Gen. Lewis A. Armistead, July 3, 1863
1994
Oil on canvas
22 x 34 inches
Collection: Hammer Galleries

Confederate Christmas (Pages 140–41)
1992
Oil on canvas
28 x 48 inches
Collection: F&M Bank, Winchester, Virginia

The Bloody Angle (Pages 5, 148–49)
Spotsylvania, Virginia, May 12, 1864
1991
Oil on canvas
24 x 36 inches
Collection: Hammer Galleries

The High Water Mark (Pages 134–35)
Gettysburg, July 3, 1863
1988
Oil on canvas
34 x 56 inches
Collection: Mr. and Mrs. Harold Bernstein

Gen. Ulysses S. Grant
(Page 142)
United States
1990
Oil on board
10 x 11½ inches
Collection:
Hammer Galleries

Thunder in the Valley (Pages 150–51)
Battle of New Market, Virginia, May 15, 1864
1992
Oil on canvas
26 x 40 inches
Collection: Goldsmith, Agio, Helms and Company

Southern Stars (Pages 152–53)
Kernstown, Virginia, Winter 1862
1994
Oil on canvas
28 x 40 inches
Collection: Mr. J. P. Darlington

Shenandoah Sunrise (Pages 156–57)
Battle of Cedar Creek, October 19, 1864
1993
Oil on canvas
28 x 46 inches
Collection: F&M Bank, Winchester, Virginia

"We Still Love You, General Lee" (Pages 164–165)
Appomattox, Virginia, April 9, 1865
1992
Oil on canvas
54 x 88 inches
Collection: Hammer Galleries

Gen. John Brown Gordon (Page 154)
Georgia
1990
Oil on board
10 x 11½ inches
Collection: Dr. Gary LeFleur

The Last Rally (Pages 158–59)
Sayler's Creek, Virginia, April 6, 1865
1991
Oil on canvas
22 x 34 inches
Collection: Mrs. Martha B. Stimpson

The Final Visit (Page 166)
Robert E. Lee, Lexington, Virginia
1995
Oil on canvas
16 x 20 inches
Collection: Hammer Galleries

". . . Cross Over the River" (Page 162)
Gen. Stonewall Jackson
1995
Oil on canvas
24 x 32 inches
Collection: Hammer Galleries

CHRONOLOGY

(Unless otherwise specified, all place names are in Virginia)

1807	January 19	Lee born at Stratford
1824	January 20	Jackson born at Clarksburg (now West Virginia)
1829	July	Lee graduates number two in West Point class
1846	July	Jackson graduates seventeenth of fifty-nine in West Point class
		Start of fourteen-month Mexican War
1851	August	Jackson begins professorship at the Virginia Military Institute
1852	September 1	Lee appointed superintendent of West Point
1859	October 17–18	Lee commands troops who quell John Brown's raid at Harpers Ferry (now West Virginia)
1861	April 20	Lee resigns from U.S. Army
	April 21	Jackson leads VMI cadets to Richmond to serve as drillmasters
	April 23	Lee accepts command of all Virginia forces
	April 26	Colonel Jackson appointed post commander at Harpers Ferry
	July 4	Jackson receives brigadier general's commission
	July 21	Victory and the name "Stonewall" come to Jackson at First Manassas (First Bull Run)
	August 31	Lee appointed full general in Confederate armies; serves as informal adviser to President Davis
	October 7	Jackson promoted to major general
	November 4	Jackson departs main army for command of Shenandoah Valley defenses
1862	January 1–10	Romney campaign (West Virginia) by Jackson brings mixed results
	March 23	Jackson's Valley campaign begins with repulse at Kernstown
	May 8	Confederate victory at McDowell
	May 25	Winchester regained by Jackson
	June 1	Lee assigned to command Army of Northern Virginia
	June 8–9	Climax of Valley campaign with Jackson victorious at Cross Keys and Port Republic
	June 12–15	Stuart's "Ride Around McClellan"
	June 25	Opening of Seven Days Battles, Lee's counteroffensive against McClellan
	June 26	Confederates defeated at Mechanicsville (Beaver Dam Creek)

	June 27	Lee and Jackson win battle of Gaines' Mill
	July 1	Lee's attacks repulsed at Malvern Hill, but Seven Days ends in victory for Confederates
	August 9	Jackson defeats Federals at Cedar Mountain
	August 29	Jackson withstands assaults at Second Manassas (Second Bull Run)
	August 30	Attack by all of Lee's army at Second Manassas sends Union army in retreat
	September 5	Confederate forces cross Potomac River on first invasion of the North
	September 15	Jackson captures garrison at Harpers Ferry
	September 17	Bloodiest day in American history at Sharpsburg (Antietam), Maryland
	October 10	Jackson promoted to lieutenant general and command of the Second Corps
	December 13	Lee's easiest victory of the war at Fredericksburg
1863	May 1–6	Confederates turn Federal advance into retreat at Chancellorsville
	May 2	In the darkness of the first night's action, Jackson accidentally shot by his own men
	May 10	Jackson dies at Guiney Station
	May 15	Jackson buried at Lexington
	June 9	Largest cavalry battle of the war at Brandy Station
	July 1	Confederates make successful gains in first day's fighting at Gettysburg
	July 2	Federals repulse assaults on both flanks
	July 3	Failure of Pickett's charge spells defeat for Lee's army at Gettysburg
	October 14	A. P. Hill's attacks at Bristoe Station meet bloody defeat
1864	May 5–6	Lee gains hard-earned victory at the battle of the Wilderness
	May 8–21	U. S. Grant's pounding at Spotsylvania successfully met by Lee
	May 15	Confederate victory at New Market
	June 3	Near massacre of Union army at Cold Harbor
	June 18	Federal siege of Richmond and Petersburg begins
	October 19	Early Confederate success at Cedar Creek turns into stunning setback
1865	April 2	Union army breaks Lee's lines at Petersburg
	April 6	Lee loses a fourth of his army at Sayler's Creek
	April 9	Surrender of Confederate army at Appomattox Court House
	August 24	Lee accepts presidency of Washington College
1870	October 12	Lee dies in Lexington
	October 15	Burial of Lee in Washington College chapel
	Late October	Name of school changed to Washington and Lee University
1883	Spring	Valentine statue of reclining Lee placed in chapel
1891	July 21	Dedication of Jackson statue over grave in Lexington cemetery

SELECTED READINGS

Borcke, Heros von. *Memoirs of the Confederate War for Independence.* 2 vols. 1866. Reprint in one volume, Dayton, Ohio: Morningside House, 1985.

Chambers, Lenoir. *Stonewall Jackson.* 2 vols. New York: Morrow, 1959.

Current, Richard N., ed. *Encyclopedia of the Confederacy.* 4 vols. New York: Simon & Schuster, 1993.

Dabney, Virginius. *Richmond: The Story of a City.* Garden City, N.Y.: Doubleday, 1976.

Davis, William C. *Jefferson Davis: The Man and His Hour—A Biography.* New York: HarperCollins, 1991.

Dowdey, Clifford. *The Land They Fought For: The Story of the South as the Confederacy, 1832–1865.* Garden City, N.Y.: Doubleday, 1955.

———. *Lee.* Boston: Little, Brown, 1965.

Freeman, Douglas Southall. *R. E. Lee: A Biography.* 4 vols. New York: Scribner's, 1934–35. One-volume abridgement, 1961.

———. *Lee's Lieutenants: A Study in Command.* New York: Scribner's, 1942–44.

Henderson, G. F. R. *Stonewall Jackson and the American Civil War.* 2 vols. 1898. Reprint, Secaucus, N.J.: Blue & Grey Press, 1989.

Horn, Stanley F., ed. *The Robert E. Lee Reader.* Indianapolis, Ind.: Bobbs-Merrill Co., 1949.

Hotchkiss, Jedediah. *Make Me a Map of the Valley: The Civil War Journal of Stonewall Jackson's Topographer.* Dallas: Southern Methodist University Press, 1973.

Jackson, Mary Anna. *Memoirs of "Stonewall" Jackson.* 1895. Reprint, Dayton, Ohio: Morningside Bookshop, 1976.

Künstler, Mort. *Images of the Civil War.* New York: Gramercy, 1992.

———. *Gettysburg.* Atlanta: Turner Publishing, 1993.

McPherson, James M. *Battle Cry of Freedom: The Civil War Era.* New York: Oxford University Press, 1988.

Marshall, Charles. *An Aide-de-Camp of Lee.* Boston: Little, Brown, and Co., 1927.

Robertson, James I., Jr. *"Civil War!" America Becomes One Nation.* New York: Knopf, 1992.

———. *General A. P. Hill: The Story of a Confederate Warrior.* New York: Random House, 1987.

———. *The Stonewall Brigade.* Baton Rouge: Louisiana State University Press, 1963.

Roland, Charles P. *An American Iliad: The Story of the Civil War.* Lexington: University Press of Kentucky, 1991.

Taylor, Walter H. *General Lee: His Campaigns in Virginia, 1861–1865.* 1906. Reprint, Dayton, Ohio: Morningside Bookshop, 1975.

Thomas, Emory M. *Bold Dragoon: The Life of J. E. B. Stuart.* New York: Harper & Row, 1986.

———. *Robert E. Lee: A Biography.* New York: W. W. Norton, 1995.

Vandiver, Frank M. *Mighty Stonewall.* New York: McGraw-Hill, 1957.

Wiley, Bell Irvin. *The Life of Johnny Reb: The Common Soldier of the Confederacy.* Indianapolis, Ind.: Bobbs-Merrill Co., 1943.

INDEX